# Programming

## *Computer Programming for Beginners*
## *Learn the Basics of Java, SQL & C++*

**By: Joseph Connor**

**4th Edition (2017)**

has been made to provide accurate, up to date and reliable complete information. No warranties of any kind are expressed or implied. Readers acknowledge that the author is not engaging in the rendering of legal, financial, medical or professional advice.

By reading this document, the reader agrees that under no circumstances are we responsible for any losses, direct or indirect, which are incurred as a result of the use of information contained within this document, including, but not limited to, — errors, omissions, or inaccuracies.

## About MJG Publishing

MJG Publishing is an independent publisher focusing on non-fiction books. Our eBooks and paperback books are targeting to help individuals to upgrade their careers & lifestyle. Learn new skills & abilities. Find the job of your dreams or create your own freelancing opportunity!

## Contact:

Visit our website: www.mjgpublishing.com

Email us: marco@mjgpublishing.com

Follow our Social Media:

Facebook: https://www.facebook.com/mjgpublishing/

Twitter: https://twitter.com/MJG_Publishing

Instagram: https://www.instagram.com/mjgpublishing/

Feel free to contact us at any time and I'll personally reply to you.

Marco J. Grishaber, MJG Publishing on behalf of Joseph Connor.

Want to Learn more about Programming?

Check out the other books by Joseph Connor:

**Newest release (2017): Programming: Computer Programming For Beginners: Learn the Basics of SQL**

**C#: Computer Programming for Beginners: Learn the Basics of C Sharp Programming – 3rd Edition (2017)**

Programming: Computer Programming For Beginners: Learn The Basics Of HTML5, JavaScript, & CSS

Python: The Definitive Guide to Learning Python Programming for Beginners

PROGRAMMING
COMPUTER PROGRAMMING
FOR BEGINNERS
Learn the Basics of Python

JOSEPH CONNOR

**Hacking: Hacking for Beginners - Computer Virus, Cracking, Malware, IT Security**

Check out our **Facebook** and **Instagram** to receive updates on the newest releases!

# Contents

# Free Video Course: Introduction to JavaScript, SQL & C++

Welcome to the journey into the world of programming. Hi I'm Marco from MJG Publishing, I wanted to thank you for supporting this book.

You're going to learn the 3 most in demand programming languages with step-by-step real examples: JavaScript, SQL, and C++.

If you study only ONE of those you can have a good career in programming. Study all three of these and you will be highly desired and in demand

Click this link: **http://www.mjgpublishing.com/free-programming-course NOW** and get immediate access to your free video series!

Find out on real examples which language suits you best and get access to our free BONUS. Receive access to code examples, learn about how to set up the different environments that you can use for programming and receive a step-by-step programming tutorial that you can put immediately into action at home.

Access this FREE video course **here**!

Happy coding,
Marco

# Introduction

Welcome to the world of computer programming, or the act of writing a program to tell your computer what to do. Programs are written using a series of instructions in a particular language, three of which I will be talking about here – Java, SQL and C++.

Computer programming is not as difficult as it first looks and it can be a lot of fun, so long as you do it properly. I have prepared a basic "Hello, World!" tutorial for each of the three languages, just to give you an idea of how it all works. Apart from this, I have also enclosed some useful tips for beginners and the common mistakes which they tend to make while programming. There is a special section at the end of the book on the frequently asked questions based on all three computer programming languages so as to make the concepts more clear.

This is aimed at people with little to no experience at programming or for those who have jumped in and are struggling to make anything work. I am confident that this book will give you an idea of how to go about learning the language of computer programming and you will be able to have a go that programming in your chosen language, moving on to more advanced coding.

Without further ado, let's get started!

# Chapter 1
# What is a Computer Program?

As I said earlier, a computer program is nothing more than a sequence of instructions that have been written with a computer programming language, telling a computer what to do. Let's take a closer look at two important terms that I used here:

- Sequence of instructions

- Computer Programming Language

In order to best understand these terms, you need to put yourself into an imaginary situation. Someone has asked you how to get to the nearest KFC restaurant. What would you tell that person?

Using human language, you would say something like "go straight for ½ a kilometer, turn left at the traffic lights and drive for one kilometer. KFC is on the right".

So, that is instructions given in English language and if followed in sequence, the person will reach KFC:

- Go straight

- Drive for ½ a kilometer

- Go left at the lights

- Drive for one kilometer

- Look for KFC on the right

Now, let's try to imagine that same situation with a computer program. What the above sequence, is a human program that instructs a person how to reach KFC. The same could have been done in any language; we chose English. The same can also be done with the computer programming language; we just use different words.

A computer program, sometimes called software, can range from just a couple of lines right up to millions of lines, each giving instructions. Those instructions are also called source code, while computer programming is known as program coding. Without a program, a computer is nothing more than a dumping box – the program is what brings the computer to life when you switch it on.

Like the human race speaks in a variety of different languages, computer scientists have come up with a number of different ones for the purpose of writing computer programming code, such as

- Java

- C

- C++

- SQL

- Python

- PHP

- Perl

- Ruby

We will be talking about three of those later on in this book.

## What Can a Computer Program do?

These days, computer programs are used virtually everywhere, in every household, in the agricultural industry, medical, defense, communications, just about anything you can think of. Examples of computer programs include:

- MS Office Suite

- Adobe Photoshop

- Any internet browser

- Any piece of software you use on your computer

- In special effects for movies

- In hospitals, in scanners, x-ray machines, ultrasound, etc.

- In your mobile phone or tablet

Before we start learning about how to program with various computer languages. Please keep the following points in mind –

1. Computer programming is all about logic and not Math. Logic in computer programming means that ability to pass through, understand the order in which things will occur and having a sense of how to control that flow.

2. Programming works on the 'holding onto' principle. If you are creating something with a process, you need to have a firm hold on it; otherwise, you are going to lose it.

3. It is always better to get a good grasp on the computer 'dictionary' before you begin programming. Most of the programming is about working to find out the best format to structure a data, and keywords of the programming language become a vital aspect in the whole process.

4. Programming is like 'Russian dolls', it is full of instances of things within things. The structures in programming often have nested structures within themselves. So when you start writing scripts, you will have to perform one thing inside other quite frequently. Therefore, getting relaxed doing these things within things is a big part of the programming learning curve.

5. In programming, you will hear lot of references to 'input' and 'output'. This is because often programming is a task to take an input of data and process it to generate an output. The

processes used are governed by codes which you will write and the data is nothing else but a file that you will work with.

6. Computer programming is based on causation principle. When you start coding, you learn how to apply the methodology to establish connection in  case that changes something.

7. Programming uses a process called 'abstraction', where you keep general things separate from specific things. So when you code few basic steps remain the same and but you have to work out a way by taking into account the specific instructions which we need to process.

We hope that these points would help you to set out on a journey of computer programming.

# Chapter 2
# The Elements of a Computer Program

The English language is made of many different elements, including redefined grammar that has to be understood if you are to write English statements correctly. It also consists of other elements, like nouns, verbs, adjectives, conjunctions, prepositions, adverbs, and so on. In the same way, computer programming languages also consist of a number of different elements, including:

- Programming Environment

- Basic Syntax

- Data Types

- Variables

- Keywords

- Basic Operators

- Decision Making

- Loops

- Numbers

- Characters

- Arrays

- Strings

- Functions

- File I/O

## How to Set Up Your Environment?

Although this is not an element of actual computer programming, it is a vital part of the entire setup and is the first thing you should do. When I talk about environment, I am talking about the base from which you intend to carry out the programming. For this, you will need:

- A PC

- A working internet connection that is a good speed

- A web browser – Internet Explorer, Chrome, Mozilla, etc.

You will need to download one of the following programs, depending on which language you are intending to program with:

- SQL

- Java

- C++

**You will also need:**

- A text editor to write your code in – Notepad or Notepad++ sre good ones – NOT Microsoft Word as it can't be read by the programming languages

- A compiler to turn your written code into binary so it can be understood

- An interpreter to directly execute your program

The latter two are usually included with the programming language download. Full instructions for setting up the programs for first use can be found on the internet.

## What is a Text Editor?

A text editor is a piece of software in which you write your computer programming code. Windows computers have Notepad installed as standard and this is perfectly OK to use. To locate and launch Notepad, click on Start, All Programs, Accessories, Notepad. Double click to open it.

Once you have typed your computer program into Notepad, you can save it to any location, as long as you remember where it is. If you use a Mac, you will have software called TextEdit installed.

## What is a Compiler?

When you have written your program using Notepad or TextEdit, or whichever text editor you choose, you will need a compiler to translate it. This is because the computer does not recognize your code in text format so it must be converted to binary – the computer is easily able to read binary.

The compiler is responsible for this conversion – without it, you will not be able to execute your program and you will not see it running on your computer.

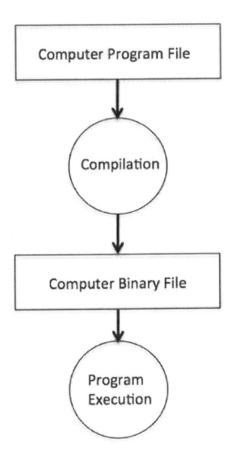

So, make sure you have the correct compiler for your chosen programming language before you start.

## What is the Interpreter?

Following the compiler, we have the interpreter, which is responsible for executing the binary code that has just been produced from your written text program. Not all compute programming languages need a compiler; they can go straight to the interpreter, which can then read the code you have written one line at a time and execute it without any further need for any work.

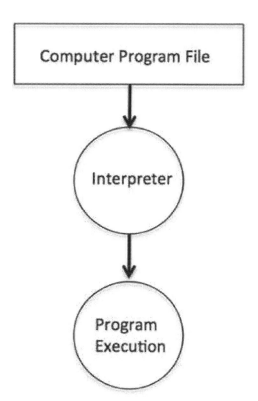

As with the compiler, make sure you have the correct interpreter installed for the language you are intending to use.

# Chapter 3
# The Pros and Cons of C++, Java, and SQL

As you now know the basics of setting up an environment for programming in C++, Java, and SQL. Let us understand the advantages and disadvantages of learning these three programming languages before we go into the details of each one of them-

## C++

C++ is an object-oriented language and is much easier to use when compared to other languages. It has many advantages when it comes to computer programming. We have listed them below –

Advantages

1. It is a highly portable language and is often considered as language of choice for multi device, multi-platform app development.

2. It is useful for low level programming and is very efficient for general purposes. It offers performance and memory efficiency.

3. Since it is an object-oriented language, it includes classes, data abstraction, inheritance, polymorphism and

encapsulation.

4. It has a rich function library.

5. The language allows exception handling and function overloading which is not there in C language. (Batra, 2016)

6. It is an efficient and fast language and finds wide range of applications such as 3D graphics for games, GUI applications to real-time mathematical simulations.

7. It is compatible with C

8. C++ has reusability of code.

Disadvantages

1. C++ gets complex in very high level programming.

2. It is commonly used for platform specific application.

3. C++ language can't support garbage collection.

4. It is not very secure language.

## JAVA

Java is one of the most popular programming languages. It is a general-purpose computer programming language and has many advantages.

Advantages

1. Java is easy to use, write and compile and debug as compared to other programming languages. It is much

similar than C++ because it uses automatic memory allocation and garbage collection.

2. It allows you to create modular programs and reusable code. (Thakker, 2016)

3. Java is platform independent, i.e. it has ability to move easily from one computer system to other.

4. Java has been designed to make distributed computing easy with the network capability that is basically integrated into it.

5. Java compiler, interpreter and runtime environment have been developed with security in mind.

6. It has a stack allocation system that helps the data to be stored and restored easily.

7. Java is multithreaded, i.e. it can perform multiple tasks simultaneously within a program.

8. Java has large number of open-source libraries

9. Java has an extensive community

Disadvantages
1. Java is slower and more memory consuming programming language when compared to C and C++.

2. Its compiler is not well optimized when compared to C++.

3. There is lack of templates which limits the ability of Java to create high quality data structures.

4. Memory management is little expensive

5. One can find some bugs in browsers

## SQL
Advantages

1. SQL offers high speed. The SQL queries can be used to retrieve large amounts of records from a database efficiently and quickly. (Gananathan)

2. SQL has well defined standards. The SQL database use long-established standards, which are adopted by ANSI & ISO. (R4R)

3. By using standard SQL, it becomes easier to manage database systems without having to write large amount of codes.

4. It is a portable language. It is run in programs in mainframes, laptops, PC's, servers and even mobile phones.

5. Databases using SQL can be moved from one device to another without any problems.

6. SQL is used by all the vendors who develop DBMS. (Thakker, 2016)

7. It is widely used for relational databases.

8. It is an easy to learn language since it mainly consists of English statements and easy to learn and understand too.

9. It is an interactive language and can be used to communicate with the databases and one can get answers to complex questions in seconds.

10. It is used for linking front end computers and back end databases. Therefore, providing client server architecture.

11. It supports object based programming and is very flexible.

12. It can integrate with JAVA by using an API (Application Programming Interface) known as JDBC (Java database connectivity).

Disadvantages

1. Interfacing an SQL database is more complex.

2. Although SQL databases conform to ISO & ANSI standards, but some databases go for proprietary extensions to standard SQL, to ensure vendor lock-in.

| C language | C++ language |
| --- | --- |
| C is a structured programming language. | C++ is an object-oriented programming language. |
| It does not support functions with default arguments | It supports ( ) with default arguments. |
| C language does not have inline function | It supports inline function. |
| It does not have exception handling | It has exception handling |
| It is a middle level language | It is a high level language |
| It has pointers | It has references and pointers |
| scanf( ) and printf( ) functions are used for standard input and output. | Cin>> and cout<< functions are used for standard input and output. |
| Program files are saved with .C extensions | Program files are saved with .CPP extensions. |

You are now ready to begin programming. For each of the three languages – C++, Java and SQL, I am going to show you how to write and produce the famous "Hello, World!" sample

# Chapter 4
# Reserved Keywords

All computer programming languages have a list of reserved keywords, words that are built in to the language for use by the language, and cannot be used as any form of identifier, such as a variable.

## Why reserved words?

The reason why a programming language reserves words is to make things easier for the compiler.

## Why not reserved words?

The downside of keeping reserve words in any programming language is that programmers do not Ray Toal, professor of computer science at MLU in Los Angeles says, "get the freedom to choose their own identifiers. It is the compiler's job to figure out when words are used in a particular context." This gets annoying sometimes for the programmers. Toal continues to say, "As a language evolves, the addition of new reserved words will break the old code." (Toal, 2010)

## How are the reserved words reserved?

When a language specifies that certain words are reserved, it typically means either of the following –

1. Toal explains that under any circumstance, that word cannot be used as a name for any programmer- defined entity (for example – a constant, variable, type, function, object property name, method, statement label, function parameter etc.) (Toal, 2010)

2. That "word can be used to name some programmer- defined entities, but its position in the source code text is restricted to simplify language processing," says Toal. (Toal, 2010)

The following lists are the reserved keywords for C language, Java and SQL – get to know them because using them out of place can result in serious errors:

**C Language Reserved Keywords**

- auto

- break

- case

- char

- const

- continue

- default

- do

- double

- else

- enum

- extern

- float

- for

- goto

- if

- int

- long

- register

- return

- short

- signed

- sizeof

- static

- struct

- switch

- typedef

- union

- unsigned

- void

- volatile

- while

- _Packed

Basic uses of these reserved words in C language are as follows –

- **break** – used with any loop OR switch case

- **if, else, switch, case** – these are used for decision control programming structure

- **int, float, char, double, long** – they are the data types and are used during variable declaration.

- **void** – it is one of the return type.

- **for, while, do** – these are types of loop structures in C.

- **goto** – it is used for redirecting the flow of execution.

- **return-** it is used for returning a value.

- auto, signed, const, extern, register, unsigned – these reserved words define a variable.

- **continue** – this keyword is typically used with for, while and dowhile loops. It performs the next iteration of the loop when compiler encounters this statement. It skips rest of the statements of current iteration.

- **sizeof** – this keyword is used to know the size.

- **enum** – it is the set of constants.

- **struct, typedef** – both these words are used in structures i.e. grouping of data types in a single record.

- **union** – this is a collection of variables, which shares the same memory storage and memory location.

(Singh)

## Java Programming Reserved Keywords
- abstract

- assert

- boolean

- break

- byte

- case

- catch

- char

- class

- const

- continue

- default

- do

- double

- else

- enum

- extends

- final

- finally

- float

- for

- goto

- if

- implements

- import

- instanceof

- int

- interface

- long

- native

- new

- package

- private

- protected

- public

- return

- short

- static

- strictfp

- super

- switch

- synchronized

- this

- throw

- throws

- transient

- try

- void

- volatile

- while

The keywords **goto** and **const** are reserved by Java. However, they are not currently used in Java. This might allow Java compiler to produce error messages if these C++ reserved words incorrectly appear in a Java program.

The following table gives description about all reserved identifiers in Java. Reserved identifiers cannot be used in any other way within the Java programs; especially you cannot use any of these reserved identifiers as your own identifiers.

| Identifier | Context | Description |
|---|---|---|
| abstract | Class modifier | Abstract class *MyAbstractClass {members;}* <br><br> Class cannot be cannot be instantiated directly, i.e. you may not "newMyAbstractClass ( )" <br> Abstract classes generally have at least one abstract method but that is not the requirement. The abstract classes may have mix of both concrete and abstract methods, or else they may have all concrete methods. |
|  | Method modifier | abstract *void aProcedure( );* <br> There is no body associated with method. A semicolon marks the end of the method. Classes that contain abstract methods must themselves be abstract. Though it is not required for abstract classes to have any abstract methods. |

| assert | | |
|--------|--------|--------|
| boolean | Primitive type | Boolean true or false<br><br>These can only be assigned value as either true or false |
| break | These are control statements which are found in iteration or switch statements. | break;<br><br>This always ends the innermost control structure in which the break statement is ended. The iteration statements do not test to see if they should execute another cycle.<br>break *label*;<br><br>The labeled break statement end all nested control structures out to the iterations or switch statement with the same label. |

|  |  | end all nested control structures out to the iterations or switch statement with the same label. |
|---|---|---|
| case | It is the switch statement clause | case CASEVALUE: *statements*; break; |
|  |  | Inside the switch statement, until a case value that matches the switch expression is found , the execution is suspended. |
| byte | It is primitive type | byte *tensOfThings*; 8-bit integer values between -128 and 127 are assigned to byte variables. |
| char | It is primitive type | char *aVowel*; These variables can be assigned 16-bit Unicode characters. |

| | | |
|---|---|---|
| catch | It handles exceptions; try statement clause | try { *statements;* }<br>catch (MyException e) { *statements;* }<br>Catch statements can only be used in conjunctions with a try statement. So when an exception is thrown in the try block of a try statement, the execution of the program continues in a catch block which matches the exception thrown. A catch block handles any exception thrown by code within a try block. |
| const | Unused | **final** is used to indicate fields that are not changed after initialization. |

| default | It is switch statement clause | default: *statements*;<br><br>In a switch statement, if none of the case clauses match the switch expression, statement execution within the switch block begins at the "default label" or "default case". |
|---|---|---|
| continue | found in iteration statements | • continue;<br>• continue looplabel;<br>**continue** statement returns to the beginning of an embedded loop, at this time the loop tests itself whether to execute the body again or exit. Labeled **continue** goes to the beginning of the iteration statement with that label. Whereas, the unlabeled **continue** goes to the beginning of the innermost nested loop |

| do | Iteration statement | do *statement*; *while (test)*; While the *while* condition is true, it executes a sequence of statements. The iterated statements are executed at least once. |
|---|---|---|
| else | If statement clause | if *(test) statement1*; *else statement2*; *else* keyword is used only in conjunctions with an **if** statement. The block or statement that follows the **else** is executed when **if** test evaluates to **false**. |
| double | It is primitive type | double *astronomicalQuantity*; 64-bit double-precision floating-point values can be assigned to double variables. |
| enum | Programmer-defined type | |
| false | It's a Boolean literal | boolean allPetsAreCats = *false*; |

| extends | Interface/ class declaration clause | • interface Secondinterface extends FirstInterface { *members;* } <br>• class MySubClass **extends** FirstInterface { members; } <br>In case a class does not explicitly extend a superclass, the class is taken to be a subclass of the class object. |
|---|---|---|
| final | class modifier | • final class NeverSuper { members; } <br>A class that can never be extended is declared by this. |
| | field modifier | • final *intLIMIT = 100;* <br>It declares a constant. |
| | method modifier | • final voidaProcedure( ) { statements; } <br>It declares a class that can never be overridden in a subclass. |

| float | It is a primitive type | float *aFloat*;<br>32-bit single precision IEEE floating point values can be assigned to float variables. |
|-------|------------------------|----------------------------------------------------------------------------------------------------------|
| finally | try statement clause | try { *statements;*}<br>finally { *statements;*}<br>Whether or not an exception was thrown in a try block, the finally block is executed. However, it is not possible to determine within the finally block whether an exception was thrown in a try block or not. |
| for | It is an iteration statement | for ( *initialize; test; update* ) *statement*;<br>While a test condition is true; it executes a statement or block. |

| if | It is a selection statement | if *(test) statement;* |
|---|---|---|
| | | It creates an option execution path. The blocks or statement is executed only if *test* evaluates to true. |
| | | if *(test) statement1;* else *statement2;*<br><br>An alternative execution path is created. If test value is evaluated to true then *statement1* is executed, otherwise *statement2* is executed. |
| goto | Unused | Only continue, return, break and throw are permitted to disrupt structured flow. |

| implements | Class declaration clause | • class        MyClass **implements** MyInterface        { members;} <br> In case an interface is implemented by a class, then it guarantees to define all the methods specified in the interface. |
| | | • class        MyClass implements FirstInterface, SecondInterface        { members; } <br> More than one interface may be implemented by a class. In this case the interface are separated by commas in the class declaration. |

| instanceof | operator | if (anObject instanceof MyClass) statement; It establishes whether the left-hand argument is an instance of a interface or named class or an instance of a subclass of the named interface/class. It evaluates either true or false. |
|---|---|---|
| import | Statement | import *package.class; import package.\*;* *It lets you access interfaces and classes that have created already, especially the Java standard class.* |
| int | it is primitive type | int *hundredsOfMillionsOfThings;* 32-bit integer values may be assigned to int variables. |
| long | it is primitive type | long *billionsOfBillionsOfThings;* 64-bit integer values may be assigned to long variables. |

| interface | Interface declaration | interface *MyInterface* { *members;* }<br>It is a specification of the methods which a class must in order to implement the interface. |
|-----------|----------------------|-----------------------------------------------------------------------------------------------------------------------------------|
| native | It is a method modifier | native *void aProcedure* ( );<br>It identifies methods that have bodies implemented outside the Java class. |
| null | It is a reference literal | *MyClass variable=null;*<br>It is the reference value that does not include any object. The null value in assignment is compatible with all reference variables. |

| new | Operator | • *MyClass variable=new MyClass ( );* |
|-----|----------|--------------------------------------|
|     |          | It creates a new instance of class |
|     |          | • *MyInterface variable=new MyInterface ( ) { members; };* |
|     |          | It creates an instance of an anonymous class that is assignment compatible with the named interface/class reference variables. |
|     |          | • *int [ ] anArray= new int[5];* |
|     |          | It allocates memory for an array. |
|     |          | There is no delete, free or destructor mechanism within Java language. The Objects become subject to garbage collection when they are no longer referenced anywhere. In Java, all instances have a predefined but not reserved method i.e. *finalizer ( )*, that is called before the garbage collection. However, there is no mechanism for forcing destruction. |

| package | statement | package *mypackage;* It declares the classes defined within the Java source file as part of a named package. With the help of *import* statement, packages can be used by other source files as well. |
|---|---|---|
| protected | It is a member scope modifier | protected *voidaProcedure( );* The protected members may be referenced within the class in which they have been declared, the classes can be in the same package, or subclasses. |
| private | Member scope modifier | private *int aField;* The private members may only be referenced within the class in which they are defined. |

| public | interface/class scope modifier | • public *interface MyInterface { members; }* |
| | | • public *class MyClass { members; }* |
| | | The public interfaces and classes may be referenced outside the package in which |
| | Member scope modifier | the class is declared. |
| | | • public *int getField( ) { statements; }* |
| | | The public members of public class may be referenced outside the package in which they are declared. |
| short | It is primitive type | short *thousandsOfThings;* 16-bit integer values may be assigned to short variables |

| return | Control statement | • *return*; Exits from a void method. This statement is optional in a void method. In case this statement is not present, the void method will still exit when it reaches the end of the method body. |
| | | • return *expression*; it exits a method that returns a value. |

| static | Member modifier | static *int numberOfInstances;* It associates members with the class and not with the individual instances. Static variables are shared between all the instances of a class unlike 'instance variables', for which each instance has an independent value. |
| | | static *void aStacticProcedure ( ) { members; }* The static methods may not refer to instance variables and may be invoked using the class name instead on an instance of the class. |

| super | class reference | • *super ( )*;<br>It invokes the constructor of a parent class from the constructor of a subclass. It should be the first executable statement within a constructor.<br><br>• *super.method ( )*<br>It invokes a method of the parent class that may have been overridden in the subclass. |
|-------|-----------------|---------------------|
| strictfp | It was added in Java 2 class/interface/member modifier | strictfp *double accountBalance*;<br>It makes sure that the floating point values are normalized during calculation rather than when just assigned to floating point variables. |

| Switch | It is a selection statement | switch (expression) |
|---|---|---|
| | | { |
| | | cases; // see case |
| | | optional_default_case; // see default |
| | | } |
| | | Switch provides multiple entries into a sequence of statements. |
| | | Switch expression (integer or character) is evaluated and the statement following the case label that matches the value is executed. Successive statements are executed even if they follow the case labels. Sequence of statements continues to be executed until **continue**, **break** or **return** is executed, or in case an unhandled exception is thrown. |
| | | Statements following the **default** label are executed in **case** no case matches the expression value. |

| this | It is a reference variable | *aComponent.addListener(this);* *this*, is a predefined reference variable defined for all non-static methods in a class. A reference to the object whose method was called is provided by it. |
|------|---------------------------|-----------------------------------|

| synchronized | Method modifier | • synchronized *voidaProcedure ( )* *{ statements; }* Synchronized methods of a class can only be executed by a single thread. In a class, threads that invoke synchronized method when another thread is executing, a synchronized method will be stopped until the thread that acquired the "lock" on the class releases the lock. |
| --- | --- | --- |
| | | • synchronized *(reference)* *statement;* Before a statement is executed a thread will wait until a lock is acquired on the reference. A lock can only be acquired for any given object by a single thread at a time. |

| throw | statement (exceptions) | throw *new Exception( )*;<br>It interrupts all parent structures and methods out to innermost **try** statement, and the current sequence of statements which are being executed. |
|-------|------------------------|-----------------------------------------------------------------------------------------------------------------------------------------------------------------------------------------------|
| transient | field modifier | transient *int temporary*;<br>Apparently, transient identifies fields that are not "persistent" when the object is saved or "serialized". Although in Java, there is nothing that takes advantage of this feature. |

| | | |
|---|---|---|
| throws | Method header clause (exceptions) | *void aProcedure( ) throws Exception* <br> *{ statements; }* <br> It identifies a procedure that either throws an exception directly, or does not handle the exception when it calls another method that throws the exception. |
| true | Boolean literal | *boolean allCatsAreAnimals = true;* |
| void | Method return type substitute | void    aProcedure(    ) *{statements;}* <br> *It identifies a method that does not return a value.* |

| | | |
|---|---|---|
| try | statement(exceptions) | *try {statements: }*<br>*Catch (IOEXception e) {*<br>*statements; }*<br>*catch (Exception e) {*<br>*statements; }*<br>*finally { statements; }*<br><br>It defines a section that could throw exceptions.<br>Statements in **try** block are executed in sequence. In case an exception occurs, and the type of the catch variable matches exception class, then the statements in the **catch** block are executed, and the exception is deemed "handled". Regardless of the fact that whether an exceptions occurs or not and whether it is handled or not, the statements in the **finally** block are executed. |

| while | Iteration statement | *while (test) statement;* it executes a block or a statement repeatedly until a *test* condition is **true**. In case the *test* condition evaluates to **false** initially, the statement is not executed. |
|---|---|---|
| volatile | field modifier (threads) | *volatile int threadFlag;* It identifies a method that does not return a value. |

(Rider, 2005)

In the above table, you would have come across certain terms like loops, class, switch, statements, primitive types etc. All these are explained in the book as you progress further.

## SQL Reserved Keywords – all in capital letters

- ADD

- ALL

- ALTER

- AND

- ANY

- AS

- ASC

- AUTHORIZATION

- BACKUP

- BEGIN

- BETWEEN

- BREAK

- BROWSE

- BULK

- BY

- CASCADE

- CASE

- CHECK

- CHECKPOINT

- CLOSE

- CLUSTERED

- COALESCE

- COLLATE

- COLUMN

- COMMIT

- COMPUTE

- CONSTRAINT

- CONTAINS

- CONTAINSTABLE

- CONTINUE

- CONVERT

- CREATE

- CROSS

- CURRENT

- CURRENT_DATE

- CURRENT_TIME

- CURRENT_TIMESTAMP

- CURRENT_USER

- CURSOR

- DATABASE

- DBCC

- DEALLOCATE

- DECLARE

- DEFAULT

- DELETE

- DENY

- DESC

- DISK

- DISTINCT

- DISTRIBUTED

- DOUBLE

- DROP

- DUMMY

- DUMP

- ELSE

- END

- ERRLVL

- ESCAPE

- EXCEPT

- EXEC

- EXECUTE

- EXISTS

- EXIT

- FETCH

- FILE

- FILLFACTOR

- FOR

- FOREIGN

- FREETEXT

- FREETEXTTABLE

- FROM

- FULL

- FUNCTION

- GOTO

- GRANT

- GROUP

- HAVING

- HOLDLOCK

- IDENTITY

- IDENTITY_INSERT

- IDENTITYCOL

- IF

- IN

- INDEX

- INNER

- INSERT

- INTERSECT

- INTO

- IS

- JOIN

- KEY

- KILL

- LEFT

- LIKE

- LINENO

- LOAD

- NATIONAL

- NOCHECK

- NONCLUSTERED

- NOT

- NULL

- NULLIF

- OF

- OFF

- OFFSETS

- ON

- OPEN

- OPENDATASOURCE

- OPENQUERY

- OPENROWSET

- OPENXML

- OPTION

- OR

- ORDER

- OUTER

- OVER

- PERCENT

- PLAN

- PRECISION

- PRIMARY

- PRINT

- PROC

- PROCEDURE

- PUBLIC

- RAISERROR

- READ

- READTEXT

- RECONFIGURE

- REFERENCES

- REPLICATION

- RESTORE

- RESTRICT

- RETURN

- REVOKE

- RIGHT

- ROLLBACK

- ROWCOUNT

- ROWGUIDCOL

- RULE

- SAVE

- SCHEMA

- SELECT

- SESSION_USER

- SET

- SETUSER

- SHUTDOWN

- SOME

- STATISTICS

- SYSTEM_USER

- TABLE

- TEXTSIZE

- THEN

- TO

- TOP

- TRAN

- TRANSACTION

- TRIGGER

- TRUNCATE

- TSEQUAL

- UNION

- UNIQUE

- UPDATE

- UPDATETEXT

- USE

- USER

- VALUES

- VARYING

- VIEW

- WAITFOR

- WHEN

- WHERE

- WHILE

- WITH

- WRITETEXT

# Chapter 5
# Basic Syntax

In this chapter, we learn to write a simple code as a first step towards learning how to do computer programming. Syntax is the set of rules that defines the combination of symbols that are measured to be a fragment in that language or a structured document of that computer language. In other words, syntax refers to the grammar and spelling of a programming language.

In the beginning, understanding syntax can seem to be a daunting task but there are a lot of tools. These tools are known as IDE's or Integrated Development Environment, which can be downloaded and used to create programs. These IDE's have built-in syntax checkers that will let you know if you are writing the correct syntax or not and apart from that it also gives you hints with what it thinks you meant to write.

Let us learn a simple syntax in C language programming –

```
#include <stdio.h>

main( ) {

    /*printf( ) function to write Hello, Everyone! */

    printf ("Hello, Everyone !");
```

Basis this example we have explained basic concepts of programming with C language –

Program Entry Point- For now, just understand that the statement *#include <stdio.h>* needs to be put at the top of a C program. All the C programs start with the main function, *main( )*, followed by left curly brace, *{*. The rest of the instructions are written in between and then the closing curly brace is put. The coding part inside these two curly braces is called as the program body. Please note that left curly brace can be in the same line as *main( )* function or in the next line.

Functions – They are small units of programs which are used to carry out a specific task. In the above example, two functions *main( )* and *printf( )* are used. Here, *printf( )* is used to print an information on the computer screen whereas *main( )* serves as the entry point for the program execution. Apart from these there are various built-in functions available which can be used in executing a program depending upon the requirement.

Comments – Statements enclosed in between /*.....*/ are called as comments. These comments are used to make programs easy to understand and user friendly. These comments are completely overlooked by interpreters and compilers; hence you can use any language you want to write your program.

Whitespaces – Irrespective of any programming language you use, when you write a program various printable characters are used to prepare program statements. Examples of such printable characters are – 1,2,3....0, !, a,b,c...z, [ ], /, &, +, +, ( ), A,B,C...Z, <, >, ?, % and so on. Apart from these, there are some characters which are used very frequently but they are not visible in your program and these characters are, new lines (\n), space, tabs (\t). These are known as whitespaces. These characters are common in all programming languages and they remain invisible in your text document. (TurtorialsPoint, 2017)

A line that contains only whitespace along with a comment is known as a blank line and such line is completely overlooked by C compiler.

Semicolons – Any individual statement in C language program should end with a semicolon (;). So if you want to write the above example "Hello, Everyone!" twice, then it will be written as mentioned below –

```
#include <stdio.h>

main( ) {

    /* printf( ) function to write Hello, Everyone! */

    printf ("Hello, Everyone!" \n);

    printf ("Hello, Everyone!");

}
```

Result would be –

Hello, Everyone!

Hello, Everyone!

In the above example, we have used \n, new line character in the first printf( ) function in order to create a new line. Now, let us suppose that we do not use the new line character in the above example, then we will get the result as follows –

Hello, Everyone! , Hello, Everyone!

<u>Explanation of the program -</u>  Now let us understand how the above C program worked. Firstly, the C compiler is used to convert the above program into a binary format.  In case there is any Syntax error then it is fixed before converting into the binary format otherwise if that is not the case then it produces a binary file called **demo**. Finally, the produced binary demo is executed and the comment inside /*...*/ is printed.

**What is a Syntax Error?**

If the rules defined by the programming language are not followed, then at the time of compilation, you will get syntax errors and as a result program will not be compiled. In syntax, a single comma, dot or a semicolon matters and when writing the code you should be careful about not missing out on these small syntax. Look at the below given example where we have skipped using semicolon –

#include <stdio.h>

```
main( ) {

    printf(" Hello, Everyone!" )

 }
```

It will give us the following result –

main.c : In function 'main' :

main.c : 7: 1: error : expected ';' before '}' token

```
}

^
```

The important thing here is that if you do not follow proper syntax as defined in the programming language, then you will get syntax errors.

This chapter would have given you a fair idea about writing a program. In the next chapter, you will learn about compiling programs in different programming languages with example and the use of basic functions with details.

# Chapter 6
# "Hello, World!"

The Hello World sample that we are all so used to seeing now is the perfect demonstration for the basic operations that are needed to create a simple CLR (common language runtime) program, to deploy it and test it. The following brief tutorials show you how to recreate the "Hello, World!" program in SQL, Java and C++.

## SQL

In order to create this project on SQL, you will need the following software:

- SQL Server or SQL Express. This can be got free from here

- AdventureWorks Database which can be downloaded from the SQL Developer Website

- .NET Framework SDK 2.0 or higher, or you can use Visual Studio 2005 or higher. .NET Framework is free to download

- The Server Instance that you are running must have CLR integration enabled

## To enable CLR integrations:

You need to have ALTER SETTINGS server level permissions.

These are implicitly held by serveradmin and sysadmin fixed server roles

Execute the following command at C:

- sp_configure 'clr enabled', 1

- GO

- RECONFIGURE

- GO

## Building "Hello World!"

- Open up the .NET Framework or Visual Studio command prompt

- Create a new directory if necessary, or just use C:/MySample

- Inside of C:\MySample (or whatever you have called it), create a new file – for Visual Basic, it should be called HelloWorld.vb and for C# it should be HelloWorld.cs

- From the code samples below, copy the right one into the right file:

- vbc C:HelloWorld.vb /target:library

- csc /target:library HelloWorld.cs

You must now compile the sample code

- Compile the code, starting at the command line prompt, by using one of the samples under the sample code heading.

- Copy the installation code from Transact-SQL into a new file and save it in the C;\MySample directory as Install.sql

- Execute the following code to deploy both the assembly and the stored procedure:

- sqlcmd -E -I -i install.sql -v root = "C:\MySample\"

- Copy the test command script from Copy Transact-SQL to a new file and save it in the C'\MySample directory as test.sql

- Use the following commend to execute the test script

- sqlcmd -E -I -i test.sql

- Copy the Cleanup script from Transact-SQL to a new file and save it in the c"\MySample directory as cleanup.sql

- Use the following command to execute the cleanup script

- sqlcmd -E -I -i cleanup.sql

## Sample Code
These are the code listings for the given sample

- C#

- using System;

```
using System.Data;

using System.Data.SqlClient;

using System.Data.SqlTypes;

using Microsoft.SqlServer.Server;

public partial class StoredProcedures

{

[Microsoft.SqlServer.Server.SqlProcedure]

public static void HelloWorld()

{

Microsoft.SqlServer.Server.SqlMetaData columnInfo

= new Microsoft.SqlServer.Server.SqlMetaData("Column1",
SqlDbType.NVarChar, 12);

SqlDataRecord greetingRecord

= new SqlDataRecord(new
Microsoft.SqlServer.Server.SqlMetaData[] { columnInfo });

greetingRecord.SetString(0, "Hello world!");

SqlContext.Pipe.Send(greetingRecord);

}
```

- };

- Visual Basic

- Imports System

- Imports System.Data

- Imports System.Data.Sql

- Imports System.Data.SqlTypes

- Imports Microsoft.SqlServer.Server

- Partial Public NotInheritable Class StoredProcedures

- <Microsoft.SqlServer.Server.SqlProcedure()> _

- Public Shared Sub HelloWorld()

- Dim columnInfo As New Microsoft.SqlServer.Server.SqlMetaData("Column1", _

- SqlDbType.NVarChar, 12)

- Dim greetingRecord As New SqlDataRecord(New _

- Microsoft.SqlServer.Server.SqlMetaData() {columnInfo})

- greetingRecord.SetString(0, "Hello World!")

- SqlContext.Pipe.Send(greetingRecord)

- End Sub

- End Class

The installation script from Transact-SQL, which deploys the assembly and created a stored procedure within the database

- USE AdventureWorks

- GO

- IF EXISTS (SELECT * FROM sys.procedures WHERE [name] = 'usp_HelloWorld')

- DROP PROCEDURE usp_HelloWorld;

- GO

- IF EXISTS (SELECT * FROM sys.assemblies WHERE [name] = 'HelloWorld')

- DROP ASSEMBLY HelloWorld;

- GO

- DECLARE @SamplesPath nvarchar(1024)

- set @SamplesPath = '$(root)'

- CREATE ASSEMBLY HelloWorld

- FROM @SamplesPath + 'HelloWorld.dll'

- WITH permission_set = Safe;

- GO

- CREATE PROCEDURE usp_HelloWorld

- --(

- @Greeting nvarchar(12) OUTPUT

- --)

- AS                         EXTERNAL                         NAME
  HelloWorld.[StoredProcedures].HelloWorld;

- GO

The Test SQL script which will execute the stored procedure and test out the sample

- use AdventureWorks

- go

- execute usp_HelloWorld

- USE AdventureWorks;

- GO

- IF EXISTS (SELECT * FROM sys.procedures WHERE [name] = 'usp_HelloWorld')

- DROP PROCEDURE usp_HelloWorld;

- GO

This Transact-SQl script will take the assembly and the stored procedure out of the database

- USE AdventureWorks

- GO

- IF EXISTS (SELECT * FROM sys.procedures WHERE [name] = 'usp_HelloWorld')

- DROP PROCEDURE usp_HelloWorld;

- GO

- IF EXISTS (SELECT * FROM sys.assemblies WHERE [name] = 'HelloWorld')

- DROP ASSEMBLY HelloWorld;

- GO

## Java

The next step is to look at how to create the same sample but using a different computer programming language – this time, Java. It takes just thee very simple steps to get this program up and running. Java is a collection of different applications, most of which are very similar to those that you are already used to using – your word processor, internet browser or email program, for example.

As you should with any application, you must ensure that you have Java installed properly on your computer system. You will also need a text editor and a terminal application for this to work.

Programming in Java

The process of building this program in Java can be broken down into three simple steps:

- Create the new program by inputting it into the text editor and saving it. Make sure you know where it is saved to and what it is called. You could, for example, call it MyProgram.java

- Compile the program by typing the following into your terminal window – javac MyProgram (or whatever yours was called).java

- Execute the program by typing the following into the terminal window – java MyProgram

The first step is creating the new program; the second converts it into characters, much like a sentence, or a poem if you like, that the computer can read and will save the output to a file called MyProgram.class and the third step is what runs the program on your computer.

## Creating the Java Program

A program is simply a character sequence, similar to a poem, a sentence or a paragraph. To create the program, all you have to do is define the sequence of characters using your text editor, in exactly the same way as you would do for an email. "Hello World!" is a good sample program to start with so type the following into your text editor and then save it as a new file called HelloWorld.java.

- public class HelloWorld {

- public static void main(String[] args) {

- System.out.println("Hello, World");

- }

- }

## Compiling the Java Program

To start with, it may look as though the Java language you are using is easily understood by the computer, but that would be incorrect. The language is actually best designed to be understood by you, the programmer. This is where the compiler comes in – it is an application that translates the language that you have written the program in into something that the computer can understand. It looks for a text file that contains the extension .java and uses that as the input and the output is a file that has a .class extension, which is the language that your computer can read and understand. To compile the HelloWorld.java file, type the following into your terminal – please note that the percentage sign (%) is used purely to denote the command prompt – yours may be different.

- % javac HelloWorld.java

Provided you type this in properly, there should not be any error messages. If there are, you need to go back and make sure the program was typed in exactly as it should have been

## Executing the Java Program

So, now that your program has been compiled, it is time to run it, or execute it. This is the most exciting bit, the part where you see the fruits of your labors. This is where the computer does what you have told it to do. To run your HelloWorld program, type the following in at your command prompt, not forgetting that the % sign should be omitted as it is only an indicator of the command prompt.

- % java HelloWorld

If everything has gone, as it should, the following should be displayed on your terminal window

- Hello, World

## Errors

If you do get any error messages, don't panic. Most errors are fixed very easily, simply by examining your code very carefully as you write it. This is the same as you would do with any Word document, fixing any spelling and grammar errors as you go.

- Compile-time Errors - These are generally caught by your computer system when you compile a program. They will stop the compiler from translating your program to a language the computer can read and it will kick up an error message that attempts to explain this to you

- Run-time Errors - These will be caught when you try to execute the program because an invalid operation is being performed, which will stop the program from running.

- Logical Errors – you should with any luck, catch these when you execute the program and a wrong answer is produced. Bugs are going to be the bane of your existence because they are tricky to find.

One of first skills that you, as a new programmer, will learn is how to identify errors. The next will be learning how to be careful when you code so you don't create any errors.

**Input and Output**

As a rule, you will want to create input for your programs. An input is data that can be processed to produce a given result. The easiest way to provide the input is shown below. When you execute the following program, it will read the argument you typed on the command line, after the name of the program and will then print it out as a part of the message:

- % javac UseArgument.java

- % java UseArgument Alice

- Hi, Alice. How are you?

- % java UseArgument Bob

- Hi, Bob. How are you?

# C++

## Structure of a C++ Program

The very best way to learn a new programming language is to get right down to it and write a program. The very first program that any new programmer will write is "Hello World!" All this program does is prints out the words, "Hello, World!" onto your screen. It is a very simple program but it also contains all of the components that are fundamental to a C++ program:

- // my first program in C++

- #include <iostream>

- int main()

- {

- std::cout << "Hello World!";

- }    Hello World!

This is the code that needs to be written for this program to be executed. So let's look at the code, one line at a time:

- Line 1: // my first program in C++

The two // at the start are an indication that the code that comes afterwards is a comment that you have put in but has absolutely no effect on the program. These tend to be included as descriptions, explanations or observations that are there for the reader's information. The computer will not read a comment. In this case, the comment is merely a description of the program.

- Line 2: #include <iostream>

Lines that start with a # are directives that are read by the preprocessor and are then interpreted. These are special lines that will be interpreted before the program is compiled. In this example, the directive that reads #include <iostream>, is telling the preprocessor that it should include a piece of C++ code that is called header iostream. This piece of code allows standard input and output operations to be performed, such as the output of writing the program, HelloWorld to your screen.

- Line 3: A blank line.

Blank lines do not mean anything special, they ae merely there to improve the readability of the stream of code.

- Line 4: int main ()

This initiates a function declaration. A function is a group of statements, in code, that are given a name. In this example, the given name is Main. While I will not go into detail on functions here, I can tell you that the definition of a function starts with a type succession, in this case int, the name, which is main and open and closed parentheses. Within these parameters can be included but that is for more advanced programming.

Main is a special function in C++ because it is the one that is called when the program is executed.

- Lines 5 and 7: { and }

Open braces indicate the start of the definition of Main and the closing brace, which you will see on line 7, indicates the end of the function. Everything that is written inside the braces is written to define the function of main when it is called. All functions begin and end with braces.

- Line 6: std::cout << "Hello World!";

This is a C++ statement. A statement is what produces the end result, the meat, if you like, what specifies the behavior. They are executed in the order that they are in within the body of the function.

This particular statement has three separate parts – std::cout; which is what identifies the standard character output device, which is usually your computer screen. The second is <<, indication that the following code is inserted into std::cout.

Lastly, the sentence that appears inside the quote marks, in this case "Hello World" is the standard output.

Note that a semicolon is used to end the statement. This always denotes the end of a statement in the same way that a full stop denotes the end of a sentence. All statements in C++ have to end with this semi-colon – failure to include it is the most common syntax error in C++ programming.

You may also have spotted that not every line of the code performs an action upon execution of the code. The lines that contain the comment (//), the directive (#) and the end of the statement (;). None of these actually performs any type of action on execution.

Sometimes you will see a computer program written with lots of indentations – while these tend to make it easier for you to read, the computer does not require any indentation or does it require the code to be written in separate lines, so it is your choice on how you write it. An example:

- int main ()

- {

- std::cout << " Hello World!";

- }

- Could have been written as:

- int main () { std::cout << "Hello World!"; }

with all the instructions in one line. This would have exactly the same meaning as the broken down example above.

In C++, you just have to remember that each statement must be separated by a semi-colon. Now, let's put another statement into your program:

- // my second program in C++

- #include <iostream>

- int main ()

- {

- std::cout << "Hello World! ";

- std::cout << "I'm a C++ program";

- } Hello World! I'm a C++ program

In this particular case, the program has performed two insertions in two different statements, both into std::cout. Again, the separation on different lines is merely to allow you to read it easier; the computer would have been just as happy with this:

- int main () { std::cout << " Hello World! "; std::cout << " I'm a C++ program "; }

The code could also have been written over more lines, as such:

- int main ()

- {

- std::cout <<

- "Hello World!";

- std::cout

- << "I'm a C++ program";

- }

The result would be exactly the same, no matter how many lines you choose to write the code over.

The preprocessor directives, the ones that start with #, are not included in the rule because they are not statements. They are simply lines of code that are read and then processed by the pre-processor before the fil is compiled. These directives must have their own line and do not need to end with a semi-colon, because they are not statements.

# Chapter 7
# What You Need to Know

No matter which programming language you opt to use, there are a number of things that you need to know. I have listed some of the common concepts that will apply to virtually every computer programming language. Have a read through and you will begin to understand what things you need to know to start leaning how to program. It might seem like a lot to learn right now but please don't worry. As you begin to program, you will learn all of the basic concepts that you need to know and each one will build on the last, until you finally have something that all comes together and makes perfect sense!

## Data Types

One of the simplest yet most important concepts in computer programming languages is a concept called data types. A data type simply represents a specific type of data that can be processed through your computer program. Data types can be alphanumeric, numeric, decimal, etc. Just as an aside from the actual computer programming, let's just step back to Math class and add up two whole numbers – a very simple process:

- 10 + 20

Nice and simple but, let's say that we want to add up two decimal numbers. This is written like this:

- 10.50 + 20.50

So, these two examples may be pretty straightforward but let's have a look at another example where we want to put some information for a student into a notebook. The following is the important information that should be recorded:

- Name:

- Class:

- Section:

- Age:

- Sex:

Now, as per the requirement, we will add in one student record:

Name: Zara Ali

- Class: 6th

- Section: J

- Age: 13

- Sex: F

So, in the first example, we looked at whole numbers and in the second one, we looked at decimal numbers, adding two of them together. The third example looked at a whole range of data. So to put that last example into computer language terms, it would describe as such:

- The student name – Zara Ali – this is a sequence of characters which is also known as a "string"

- The student class – 6th – this is represented by a mixture of whole numbers and two characters (more than one character together is called a string). This is all known as an alphanumeric data type

- The student section is represented by one single character, a "J".

- The student age – 13 – is represented by a whole number

- The student sex is represented by one single character, "F", to indicate that the student is female.

Through this, you can see that, in our daily life we are constantly dealing with different data types, such as characters, strings, whole numbers (also called integers), decimal numbers (also called floating point numbers) and alphanumeric strings.

This is similar to the way a computer program is written. In order for that program to process a range of different data types, we must ensure that the type is clearly specified otherwise the computer will not know how a range of different operations can be carried out in that specific data. Different languages will use different keywords as a way of specifying different data types. In the next section I am going to go over the use of different data types in different situations for C language, Java and SQL.

## C and Java Data types

C and Java tend to share many of the same data types, although Java does include support for extra types. The following are the common data types that both languages support:

| Type | Keyword | Value range that may be represented by this data type |
|---|---|---|
| Character | char | -128 to 127 or 0 to 255 |
| Number | int | -32,768 to 32,767 or -2,147,483,648 to 2,147,483,647 |
| Small Number | short | -32,768 to 32,767 |
| Long Number | long | -2,147,483,648 to 2,147,483,647 |
| Decimal Number | float | 1.2E-38 to 3.4E+38 till 6 decimal places |

These are all called primitive data types and they can be used in the process of building up more complex data types. The more complex ones are known as user-defined data types, for example a sequence of characters known as a string.

## SQL Data Types

In SQL, every column that is present inside a database must have a name and a data type attached to it. As the developer, it is up to you to determine what data type is going to be stored inside each of the table columns when you are creating a table in SQL. The data type is a way for SQL to understand what it should expect in terms of data inside each separate column and it also determines how SQL will interact with the data stored. These are the general data types for SQL:

| Data type | Description |
|---|---|
| CHARACTER(n) | Character string. Fixed-length n |
| VARCHAR(n)  or  CHARACTER VARYING(n) | Character string. Variable length. Maximum length n |
| BINARY(n) | Binary string. Fixed-length n |
| BOOLEAN | Stores TRUE or FALSE values |
| VARBINARY(n)  or  BINARY VARYING(n) | Binary string. Variable length. Maximum length n |
| INTEGER(p) | Integer numerical (no decimal). Precision p |
| SMALLINT | Integer numerical (no decimal). Precision 5 |
| INTEGER | Integer numerical (no decimal). Precision 10 |
| BIGINT | Integer numerical (no decimal). Precision 19 |
| DECIMAL(p,s) | Exact numerical, precision p, scale s. Example: decimal(5,2) is a number that has 3 digits before the decimal and 2 digits after the decimal |

| | |
|---|---|
| NUMERIC(p,s) | Exact numerical, precision p, scale s. (Same as DECIMAL) |
| FLOAT(p) | Approximate numerical, mantissa precision p. A floating number in base 10 exponential notation. The size argument for this type consists of a single number specifying the minimum precision |
| REAL | Approximate numerical, mantissa precision 7 |
| FLOAT | Approximate numerical, mantissa precision 16 |
| DOUBLE PRECISION | Approximate numerical, mantissa precision 16 |
| DATE | Stores year, month, and day values |
| TIME | Stores hour, minute, and second values |
| TIMESTAMP | Stores year, month, day, hour, minute, and second values |
| INTERVAL | Composed of a number of integer fields, representing a period of time, depending on the type of interval |

| | |
|---|---|
| ARRAY | A set-length and ordered collection of elements |
| MULTISET | A variable-length and unordered collection of elements |
| XML | Stores XML data |

## Variables

In programming, a variable is similar to those variables you may (or may not) remember from Algebra. Instead of simply holding a number, variable in computer programming hold numbers, text and other things.

The most commonly used types of variable are:

- Integer - a whole number, without a decimal point

- Double or Float – A number that may or may not have a decimal point

- String – quite simply, a string of characters - numbers, letters, words – written as text.

- Boolean – this variable can be set to TRUE or FALSE and is useful in executing the program controls – once you get deeper into programming

Variables are another very important concept in computer

programming. They are the names that you give the computer memory location where the values are stored inside the program. Let's say that you wanted to store two values in your program, with a view to using them later on. Let's have a look at how that is done, in just three easy steps:

- You create the variables using appropriate names – one for each value

- You store your values within those two variables

- You retrieve the stored values from the variables and use them

## Creating Variables

The act of creating a variable is also known as declaring the value in C programming. Different languages use different ways to create or declare variables in your program. An example in C language would be:

- #include <stdio.h>

- main()

- {

- int a;

- int b;

- }

This program has declared two variables – it has reserved two locations in the memory with the names "a" and "b". These have been created by using the "int" keyword, specifying the variable data type, which says that the values we want to store in the variables are integers. In the same way, using the right keywords, you can also store data in variables that are declared as "float", "long", "char" or any of the other data types. An example of this:

- /* variable to store long value */

- long a;

- /* variable to store float value */

- float b;

You can also declare variables that are similar in type by placing them on one line of code, each separated by a comma. For example:

- #include <stdio.h>

- main()

- {

- int a, b;

- }

Here are some important things you need to keep in mind about variables:

- The name of a variable is able to hold one single value type only, i.e. if a variable called "a" has been given a data type "int", it is only able to store integers

- C language needs a variable to be declared before it can be used in your program. You are not able to use any variable without declaring it in most languages, one exception to that rule being Python, which does allow you to do this

- You can only use a particular variable name once in your program. For example, if you define variable "a" as an "int", to store values that are integers, you cannot then define "a" to store any other value that is not an integer, or is any other type of data.

- Some programming languages do not want you specifying any particular data type when you create a variable. This means that you can, in some languages, store float, integer or long values without actually specifying what their data type is.

- You can name a variable anything you like, but be aware that many languages do limit you to a set number of characters per variable name. For now, stick to using the following characters in your variable names as they are accepted by all languages and begin your variable name with a letter rather than just using digits – "a-z", "A-Z", and "0-9"

- Virtually no programming language will allow you to begin your variable name with a digit so something like "2015" would not be acceptable, whereas "year2015" would be valid

There are lots more rules for variables, specific to each programming language and, as you get deeper into each language, you will learn more about them. These basic rules ae enough for you to begin with for now so let's move on to storing values.

## Store Values in Variables

Now you know how to create or declare a variable, it's time to look at how to store values in them:

- #include <stdio.h>

- main()

- {

- int a;

- int b;

- a = 10;

- b = 20;

- }

In this program, we have included a pair of additional statements. In variable "a" we are storing a value of 10 and in variable "b" we are storing a value of 20. Virtually all computer programming languages provide a similar way of doing this, where the variable name is on the left of the = (equal) sign and the value that you want to store in the variable is on the right side.

Now, we have declared two variables and we have also stored the necessary values in those variables. One variable now has a value of 10 and the other has a value of 20. This means that, when this program is executed, the memory location for "a" will hold 10 and the memory location for "b" will hold 20.

**Access Stored Values in Variables**

There is little point in going to the effort to declare a variable and store a value in t if you are not going to use that value at some point. The program above contains two variables with separate values. The next step is to try to print those values that are stored in the variables. The following example is for C language and the command we use will print those values for us:

- #include <stdio.h>

- main()

- {

- int a;

- int b;

- a = 10;

- b = 20;

- printf( "Value of a = %d\n", a );

- printf( "Value of b = %d\n", b );

- }

When we execute this program, we get this result:

- Value of a = 10

- Value of b = 20

You will have spotted that we used the "printf" function when we looked at the "Hello, World!" example. In this articular program, we are using that function to print out the values that are stored inside the variables. As well as that, we have used "%d" which will be replaced with the values that are stored in the variables that are used in the "printf" statement. Both values can be printed using the "printf" statement, as follows:

- #include <stdio.h>

- main()

- {

- int a;

- int b;

- a = 10;

- b = 20;

- printf( "Value of a = %d and value of b = %d\n", a, b );

- }

When we execute this program, we get this result:

- Value of a = 10 and value of b = 20

In C programming, if you want to make use of the float variable, you will need to use "%f" instead of "%d". If you want to print out a value, you would use "%c". In a similar manner, a range of different data types can be printed just by using "%" and different characters.

**Variables in Java**

The above was for C program so let's have a look at the equivalent program using the Java language instead. We will declare two variables, "a" and "b" and we will assign the values "10" and "20" to them as well before printing the values in two different ways:

- public class DemoJava

- {

- public static void main(String []args)

- {

- int a;

- int b;

- a = 10;

- b = 20;

- System.out.println("Value of a = " + a);

- System.out.println("Value of b = " + b);

- System.out.println("Value of a = " + a + " and value of b = " + b);

- }

- }

## Variables in SQL

In the SQL language, a variable lets the programmer store data on a temporary basis, while the code is being executed. The syntax used to declare the variables in SQL, using the statement "DECLARE", is:

- DECLARE @variable_name datatype [ = initial_value ],

- @variable_name datatype [ = initial_value ],

- ...;

## Parameters or Arguments
To break that down a little:

- The variable name is the name that you assign to that variable

- The data type is the type that is assigned to the variable, i.e. "int", "float" etc.

- The initial_value is optional and it is the value that you first assign to the variable when you declare it

Below is an example of how we declare a variable in SQL:

- DECLARE @techonthenet VARCHAR(50);

The DECLARE statement is declaring a variable that we have called "@techonthenet", which is a VARCHAR type of data, containing 50 characters. . Next, using the SET statement, we are going to change the value of @techonthenet", like this:

- SET @techonthenet = 'Example showing how to declare variable';

Next, we are going to look at how an INT variable is declared in

SQL:

- DECLARE @site_value INT;

If you want to assign a particular value to "@site_value", use the SET statement, like this:

- SET @site_value = 10;

This statement is giving a value of integer 10 to the variable

What if you wanted to declare more than one variable in SQL? You would do it like this:

- DECLARE @techonthenet VARCHAR(50),

- @site_value INT;

We have declared two variables, the first being "@techofthenet", defined as VARCHAR (50) and the second is called "site_value", defined as INT.

Now let's have a quick look at how to declare a variable and give it an initial value

- DECLARE @techonthenet VARCHAR(50) = how to declare variable';

We use the DECLARE statement to declare the "@techonthenet" statement that has been defined as data type VARCHAR, with a character length of 50. We then set the "techonthenet" variable to declare "how to declare variable" – bear in mind, this is just an example of how to do it.

Lastly, let's have a look at declaring an INT variable in SQL with an initial value:

- DECLARE @site_value INT = 10;

This declaration is declaring a variable that we called "@site_value", with an INT data type. The value of that variable is then set at an integer value of 10.

To declare more than one variable with initial values, you would do something like this:

- DECLARE @techonthenet VARCHAR(50) = 'how to declare variable',

- @site_value INT = 10;

Here, we have declared a pair of variables and each has been assigned an initial value in the declaration:

The first one, called "@techonthenet", has been defined as a VARCHAR data type with a 50 character length and has been assigned an initial value of "how to declare variable".

The second, called "@site_value", has been declared as an INT data type and has been given an integer value of 10

## Operators

Operators are used to work on the variables in your program. The most common operators are:

- + - addition

- Subtraction

- multiplication

- / - division

- = - an assignment of a value, such as X=4

- ++ - increments of an integer by 1

- subtraction from an integer by 1

In any programming language, an operator is used to tell the interpreter or the compiler to carry out particular and very specific operations, either logical, mathematical or relational, and produce an end result. We are now going to talk about some of the more important relational and operational operators that are used in C and Java languages

## Arithmetic Operators

We often use computer programs to carry out mathematical calculations and we can easily write a program that will add up two numbers, or another simple equation. We can write a program that will solve a more complex equation as well. Have a look at the following mathematical examples:

- 2 + 3

- $P(x) = x4 + 7x3 - 5x + 9$.

These are both called arithmetic expressions in the computer programming language and the + and − are called arithmetic operators. The values, such as 2, 3, and so on, are called operands. Expressions like these, in their simplest form, always produce a result that is numerical.

In a similar way, computer programming languages provide a number of different arithmetic operators. The table below shows some of the more important operators in C language. For the purposes of this book, assume that variable "A" has a value of 10 and variable "B" has a value of 20:

| Operator | Description | Example |
|----------|-------------|---------|
| + | Adds two operands | A + B will give 30 |
| - | Subtracts second operand from the first | A - B will give -10 |
| * | Multiplies both operands | A * B will give 200 |
| / | Divides numerator by de-numerator | B / A will give 2 |
| % | This gives remainder of an integer division | B % A will give 0 |

Next is an example of a program to help you understand these operators:

- #include <stdio.h>

- main()

- {

- int a, b, c;

- a = 10;

- b = 20;

- c = a + b;

- printf( "Value of c = %d\n", c);

- c = a - b;

- printf( "Value of c = %d\n", c);

- c = a * b;

- printf( "Value of c = %d\n", c);

- c = b / a;

- printf( "Value of c = %d\n", c);

- c = b % a;

- printf( "Value of c = %d\n", c);

- }

When we execute the above program, the following result is produced:

- Value of c = 30

- Value of c = -10

- Value of c = 200

- Value of c = 2

- Value of c = 0

## Relational Operators

Think of a situation that would require you to create a pair of variables and then assign then values, like this:

- A = 20

- B = 10

In this example, it is clear that the value of "A" is greater than the value of "B". But, if you wanted to write that in computer language, how would you do it? You would need to use symbols to help you write this kind of expression, called relational expressions. In C language, they would be written like this:

- (A > B)

We have used the symbol >, known as an operational operator. In its simplest form, it will produce a Boolean result, meaning that the result is not true nor is it false. The table below shows the more important relational operators in C language. Once again, assume that "A" has a value of 10 and "B" has a value of 20:

| Operator | Description | Example |
|---|---|---|
| == | Checks if the values of two operands are equal or not, if yes then condition becomes true. | (A == B) is not true. |
| != | Checks if the values of two operands are equal or not, if values are not equal then condition becomes true. | (A != B) is true. |
| > | Checks if the value of left operand is greater than the value of right operand, if yes then condition becomes true. | (A > B) is not true. |
| < | Checks if the value of left operand is less than the value of right operand, if yes then condition becomes true. | (A < B) is true. |
| >= | Checks if the value of left operand is greater than or equal to the value of right operand, if yes then condition becomes true. | (A >= B) is not true. |
| <= | Checks if the value of left operand is less than or equal to the value of right operand, if yes then condition becomes true. | (A <= B) is true. |

Next, we are going to look at an example of programming in C language that sees the "if conditional statement". This is used to check a condition – it that condition is true, the if statement body will be executed; if it is false, the statement will be skipped over.

```c
#include <stdio.h>

main()

{

int a, b;

a = 10;

b = 20;

/* Here we check whether a is equal to 10 or not */

if( a == 10 )

{

/* if a is equal to 10 then this body will be executed */

printf( "a is equal to 10\n");

}

/* Here we check whether b is equal to 10 or not */

if( b == 10 )

{

/* if b is equal to 10 then this body will be executed */

printf( "b is equal to 10\n");
```

- }

- /* Here we check if a is less b than or not */

- if( a < b )

- {

- /* if a is less than b then this body will be executed */

- printf( "a is less than b\n");

- }

- /* Here we check whether a and b are not equal */

- if( a != b )

- {

- /* if a is not equal to b then this body will be executed */

- printf( "a is not equal to b\n");

- }

- }

When we execute this program, this is the result we get:

- a is equal to 10

- a is less than b

- a is not equal to b

## Logical Operators

Logical operators hold a place of importance in all programming languages and they are used to help make decisions that are based on specific conditions. Let's say that we want to combine the result of two separate conditions. We would use two logical operators to help us get to that result – AND and OR.

The table below shows all of the logical operators that are supported in C language. Again, A has a value of 10 while B has a value of 20

| Operator | Description | Example |
|---|---|---|
| && | Called Logical AND operator. If both the operands are non-zero, then condition becomes true. | (A && B) is false. |
| \|\| | Called Logical OR Operator. If any of the two operands is non-zero, then condition becomes true. | (A \|\| B) is true. |
| ! | Called Logical NOT Operator. Use to reverses the logical state of its operand. If a condition is true then Logical NOT operator will make false. | !(A && B) is true. |

Have a look at this example, to try to help you understand how the logical operators work

- #include <stdio.h>

- main()

- {

- int a = 1;

- int b = 0;

- if ( a && b )

- {

- printf("This will never print because condition is false\n" );

- }

- if ( a || b )

- {

- printf("This will be printed print because condition is true\n" );

- }

- if ( !(a && b) )

- {

- printf("This will be printed print because condition is true\n" );

- }

- }

When you have compiled and the executed this program, the following result will be produced:

- This will be printed print because condition is true

- This will be printed print because condition is true

## Operators in Java

The following is a similar program that has been written in Java programming language. Both C and Java use a set of operators and conditional statements that are almost identical. The following program is going to declare two variables, "a" and "b" again and, in a similar way to C, we are going to assign the values of 10 and 20 to these variables. Lastly, we will make use relational and arithmetic operators.

See if you can compile and then execute this program to see what the output is. Bear in mind that it must be the same output as in the example in C programming above:

- public class DemoJava

- {

- public static void main(String []args)

- {

- int a, b, c;

- a = 10;

- b = 20;

- c = a + b;

- System.out.println("Value of c = " + c );

- c = a - b;

- System.out.println("Value of c = " + c );

- c = a * b;

- System.out.println("Value of c = " + c );

- c = b / a;

- System.out.println("Value of c = " + c );

- c = b % a;

- System.out.println("Value of c = " ı c );

- if( a == 10 )

- {

- System.out.println("a is equal to 10" );

- }

- }

- }

## Operators in SQL

Operators are reserved words or characters that are used in the WHERE clause of an SQL statement to perform one or more operations, like arithmetic and comparison operations. They are used as a way of specifying conditions in SQL statements and are also used as conjunctions for multiple conditions in statements. The following are the most common operators in SQL:

- Arithmetic operators

- Comparison operators

- Logical operators

- Operators used to negate conditions

**SQL Arithmetic Operators:**

The table below shows the SQL arithmetic operators. As before, variable "" has a value of 10 and "b" has a value of 20

| Operator | Description | Example |
|---|---|---|
| + | Addition - Adds values on either side of the operator | a + b will give 30 |
| - | Subtraction - Subtracts right hand operand from left hand operand | a - b will give -10 |
| * | Multiplication - Multiplies values on either side of the operator | a * b will give 200 |
| / | Division - Divides left hand operand by right hand operand | b / a will give 2 |
| % | Modulus - Divides left hand operand by right hand operand and returns remainder | b % a will give 0 |

## SQL Comparison Operators:

This table shows the comparison operators n SQL – "a" has a value of 10 and "b" has a value of 20

| Operator | Description | Example |
|---|---|---|
| = | Checks if the values of two operands are equal or not, if yes then condition becomes true. | (a = b) is not true. |
| != | Checks if the values of two operands are equal or not, if values are not equal then condition becomes true. | (a != b) is true. |
| <> | Checks if the values of two operands are equal or not, if values are not equal then condition becomes true. | (a <> b) is true. |
| > | Checks if the value of left operand is greater than the value of right operand, if yes then condition becomes true. | (a > b) is not true. |
| < | Checks if the value of left operand is less than the value of right operand, if yes then condition becomes true. | (a < b) is true. |
| >= | Checks if the value of left operand is greater than or equal to the value of right operand, if yes then condition becomes true. | (a >= b) is not true. |
| <= | Checks if the value of left operand is less than or equal to the value of right operand, if yes then condition becomes true. | (a <= b) is true. |
| !< | Checks if the value of left operand is not less than the value of right operand, if yes then condition becomes true. | (a !< b) is false. |
| !> | Checks if the value of left operand is not greater than the value of right operand, if yes then condition becomes true. | (a !> b) is true. |

## SQL Logical Operators:

This table shows all the logical operators used in SQL:

| Operator | Description |
| --- | --- |
| ALL | The ALL operator is used to compare a value to all values in another value set. |
| AND | The AND operator allows the existence of multiple conditions in an SQL statement's WHERE clause. |
| ANY | The ANY operator is used to compare a value to any applicable value in the list according to the condition. |
| BETWEEN | The BETWEEN operator is used to search for values that are within a set of values, given the minimum value and the maximum value. |
| EXISTS | The EXISTS operator is used to search for the presence of a row in a specified table that meets certain criteria. |
| IN | The IN operator is used to compare a value to a list of literal values that have been specified. |
| LIKE | The LIKE operator is used to compare a value to similar values using wildcard operators. |
| NOT | The NOT operator reverses the meaning of the logical operator with which it is used. Eg: NOT EXISTS, NOT BETWEEN, NOT IN, etc. This is a negate operator. |
| OR | The OR operator is used to combine multiple conditions in an SQL statement's WHERE clause. |
| IS NULL | The NULL operator is used to compare a value with a NULL value. |
| UNIQUE | The UNIQUE operator searches every row of a specified table for uniqueness (no duplicates). |

## Braces

{} – also termed curly braces. These are used as a way of controlling the program flow. Everything that is inside a pair of curly braces has to be executed as a group, not individuals

## Functions

These are also similar to those in Algebra and are used, sometimes on a variable, to do the work necessary to obtain a result.

## Include Files

Most programming languages will use this and you will normally find it at the start of a set of code. Include Files has information that is needed by the program so that it can run the code that is in the program. Instead of having all the code coped to the program (as this takes up a lot of space and can get quite complex). The compiler simply looks for the instructions it needs to execute the item that is in the Include Files plus the code you wrote.

# Basic Syntax rules
## Java and C++

Java and C++ programs are defined as a set of objects that talk to each other through methods. Let's take a brief look at what objects, class, methods and instance variables mean:

- Object – Each object has a state and a behavior. An example – a dog has colors, breeds and names, which are states, and

146

they eat, bark or wag their tails, which are behaviors. An object is an instance of a class

- Class – A class is a template that carries a description of the states and behaviors that are supported by its type

- Methods – A behavior. Classes can contain unlimited methods and they are where data manipulation, logics and execution of an action take place

- Instance variables – Every object has its own set of these and it is the values that are assigned to an instance variable that creates the state of the object.

When it comes to writing code in Java, there are some basis syntax rules you must follow:

- Case - Java is a case sensitive language. This means that the identifier "hello" would have a different meaning to the identifier "Hello"

- Class Names – All class names should begin with an upper case letter. If you use more than one word to form a class name, each word should begin with an upper case letter, for example MyFirstJavaClass

- Method Names – Method names should being with a lower case letter and, similar to class names, if more than one word is used, each word must have a lower case letter at the beginning.

- Program File Names – The name of the program file name should be exactly the same as the class name so remember that when you save it. Don't forget to use the right case and to add.java to the end of the name. If the class and the file name are not the same, your program is not going to compile.

## Java Identifiers

Every Java component has to have a name and the names that we use for variables, classes and methods are known as identifiers. You need to remember these points:

- All identifiers must start with a letter – A – Z or a – z, or they should start with an underscore (_) or a currency character

- The rest of the identifier name can be made up of any combination of different characters

- You cannot use any of the reserved keywords as identifiers

- Identifiers are case sensitive

- A few examples of identifiers that are legal are age, $wage, _value, ___1_value

- An illegal identifier would look something like 123abc, -wage

## Java Modifiers

In a similar way to other computer programming languages, you can modify methods, classes, etc. by using something called a modifier. In Java, we use two categories of modifiers:

- Access Modifiers - private, public, protected, default

- Non-Access Modifiers - abstract, final, strictfp

## Java Variables

In Java language, you will see these variable types:

- Local

- Class

- Instance

## Java Arrays

An array is an object that is used to store multiple values that are of the same type.

## Java Enums

Enums are a relatively new thing in Java and they restrict variables so that they can only have one of a small number of pre-defined values. These values are called enums. By using these, it is possible to cut down on the number of bugs that are in your code. Let's take an example here of a shop that sells fresh juice. You can restrict the size of the juice glass to small, medium or large and this would ensure that this was the only size that people could buy. An example of the code:

- class FreshJuice {

- enum FreshJuiceSize{ SMALL, MEDIUM, LARGE }

- FreshJuiceSize size;

- }

- public class FreshJuiceTest {

- public static void main(String args[]){

- FreshJuice juice = new FreshJuice();

- juice.size = FreshJuice.FreshJuiceSize.MEDIUM ;

- System.out.println("Size: " + juice.size);

- }

- }

The result from this particular example would be:

- Size: MEDIUM

It is possible to declare an enum inside a class or on its own and methods, variables and constructors can also be defined inside an enum.

**Java Comments**
The Java language supports both multi and single line comments and the Java compiler will ignore any character that is inside a comment:

- public class MyFirstJavaProgram{

- /* This is my first java program.

- This will print 'Hello World' as the output

- This is an example of multi-line comments.

- */

- public static void main(String []args){

- // This is an example of single line comment

- /* This is also an example of single line comment. */

- System.out.println("Hello World");

- }

- }

**Using Blank Lines in Java**

A line that contains nothing but white space and perhaps a comment is called a blank line and is ignored completely by Java

**Java Inheritance**

In the Java language, it is possible to derive a class from a class. Let's say that you needed to create a new class but there is already one that contains a bit of the code that you need. It is possible to derive the new class from the existing one. This allows you to use fields and methods from existing class without the need to write a new code. The original class is called the superclass and the new class that you have derived from it is called the subclass.

**Java Interfaces**

In Java, an interface is defined as a contract that sets out how objects communicate with one another. Interfaces are vital in the concept of inheritance because the interface will define the methods that the subclass uses. However, implementation of those methods is entirely up to the subclass.

**C++Semicolons and Blocks**

In the C++ language, the semicolon is used to terminate a statement and, to that end, all statements must be finished off with a semicolon, to indicate that the logical entity has ended. For example, have a look at these three statements:

- x = y;

- y = y + 1;

- add(x, y);

A block is a collection of statements that are logically connected and are enclosed in braces:

- {

- cout << "Hello World"; // prints Hello World

- return 0;

- }

C++ will not see the end of each statement as a terminator because it is not a semicolon. So, for this reason, you can put a statement anywhere on a line. For example:

- x = y;

- y = y+1;

- add(x, y);

- is exactly the same as:

- x = y; y = y+1; add(x, y);

## C++ Identifiers

These are used to identify a class, function, variable, module or any other item that is user-defined. A few points to remember about C++ identifiers:

- They must begin with a letter – A to Z or a to z, an underscore (_) that is followed by a zero or, more underscores, letters or digits (0 to 9)

- Punctuation characters such a $., @, or % are not allowed in C++ identifiers

- C++ is case sensitive, which means that, for example, Manpower is a different identifier to manpower.

**Examples of identifiers that are acceptable are:**

- Mohr

- Zara

- ABCW

- move name

- a_123

- myname50

- _temp

- j

- a23b9

- retVal

## C++ Trigraphs

Some characters have another representation in C++ and this is known as a trigraph sequence. A trigraph is a sequence of three characters, representing one single character. The sequence will always begin with a pair of question marks (??). The most common of the trigraph sequences are:

?? = replaces #

?? / replaces \

??' replaces    ^

?? ( replaces    [

??) replaces    ]

??! replaces    |

?? < replaces {

?? > replaces }

?? - replaces   ~

Not all C++ compilers will support trigraphs and, in all fairness, it is probably better that you do not use the, simply because they can be confusing. I have mentioned them because you are likely to come across them and will need to know what they are.

## C++ Whitespace

As in Java, a line that contains whitespace only, maybe with a comment is a blank line and is ignored by C++. The language uses whitespace as the term to describe tabs, banks, comments and newline characters. It is used to separate a statement into parts and allows the compiler to see where one part of a statement ends and another part begins. For example, in this statement:

- int age;

there has to be at least one whitespace character, normally a space, in between int and age so that the compiler knows to distinguish between them and can read the statement correctly. However, in this statement:

- fruit = apples + oranges;  // Get the total fruit

it isn't necessary to put in a whitespace character between fruit and = or in between = and apples. You can if you wish but it won't make any difference to the way C++ reads it

## SQL

SQL is a little different to Java and C++ and it follow a unique set of guidelines and rules. All statements in SQl have to begin with one of the keywords, such as INSERT, SELECT, CREATE, SHOW, ALTER, USE, DELETE, or UPDATE for example, and every statement must end with a semicolon

It is important to remember that SQL is NOT case sensitive, which means that SELECT and select both have the same meaning. Take a look at the following examples of SQL statements and clauses to see how they are set out:

- SELECT Statement:

- SELECT column1, column2....columnN

- FROM  table_name;

- DISTINCT Clause:

- SELECT DISTINCT column1, column2....columnN

- FROM table_name;

- WHERE Clause:

- SELECT column1, column2....columnN

- FROM table_name

- WHERE CONDITION;

- AND/OR Clause:

- SELECT column1, column2....columnN

- FROM table_name

- WHERE CONDITION-1 {AND|OR} CONDITION-2;

- IN Clause:

- SELECT column1, column2....columnN

- FROM table_name

- WHERE column_name IN (val-1, val-2,...val-N);

- BETWEEN Clause:

- SELECT column1, column2....columnN

- FROM table_name

- WHERE column_name BETWEEN val-1 AND val-2;

- LIKE Clause:

- SELECT column1, column2....columnN

- FROM table_name

- WHERE column_name LIKE { PATTERN };

- ORDER BY Clause:

- SELECT column1, column2....columnN

- FROM table_name

- WHERE CONDITION

- ORDER BY column_name {ASC|DESC};

- GROUP BY Clause:

- SELECT SUM(column_name)

- FROM table_name

- WHERE CONDITION

- GROUP BY column_name;

- COUNT Clause:

- SELECT COUNT(column_name)

- FROM   table_name

- WHERE  CONDITION;

- HAVING Clause:

- SELECT SUM(column_name)

- FROM   table_name

- WHERE  CONDITION

- GROUP BY column_name

- HAVING (arithmetic function condition);

- CREATE TABLE Statement:

- CREATE TABLE table_name(

- column1 datatype,

- column2 datatype,

- column3 datatype,

- .....

- columnN datatype,

- PRIMARY KEY( one or more columns )

- );

- DROP TABLE Statement:

- DROP TABLE table_name;

- CREATE INDEX Statement:

- CREATE UNIQUE INDEX index_name

- ON table_name ( column1, column2,...columnN);

- DROP INDEX Statement:

- ALTER TABLE table_name

- DROP INDEX index_name;

- DESC Statement:

- DESC table_name;

- TRUNCATE TABLE Statement:

- TRUNCATE TABLE table_name;

- ALTER TABLE Statement:

- ALTER TABLE table_name {ADD|DROP|MODIFY} column_name {data_ype};

- ALTER TABLE Statement (Rename):

- ALTER TABLE table_name RENAME TO new_table_name;

- INSERT INTO Statement:

- INSERT INTO table_name( column1, column2....columnN)

- VALUES ( value1, value2....valueN);

- UPDATE Statement:

- UPDATE table_name

- SET    column1   =   value1,   column2   =
  value2....columnN=valueN

- [ WHERE  CONDITION ];

- DELETE Statement:

- DELETE FROM table_name

- WHERE  {CONDITION};

- CREATE DATABASE Statement:

- CREATE DATABASE database_name;

- DROP DATABASE Statement:

- DROP DATABASE database_name;

- USE Statement:

- USE database_name;

- COMMIT Statement:

- COMMIT;

- ROLLBACK Statement:

- ROLLBACK;

**SQL Loops**

There may come a time when you will have to execute a code block repeatedly. This is called a loop. In SQL, we use the following loop types:

- SQL Basic LOOP - The statement sequence is in between LOOP and END LOOP. The sequence s executed at each iteration and control begins again at the top of the loop

- SQL WHILE LOOP - Provided a given condition is true, singe or group of statements will repeat. The condition is tested before the loop body is executed

- SQL FOR LOOP - Will perform multiple executions of a statement sequence and abbreviates the loop variable management code

- Nested loops in SQL - Allows you to use a single or multiple loops inside any other basic, WHILE, or FOR loop.

**Labeling a Loop**

SQL loops can be given a label that must be enclosed in double angle brackets (<< and >>) and should be at the beginning of the statement or at the end. Labels can be used in the EXIT statement to get out of the loop. The following shows how that works:

- DECLARE

- i number(1);

- j number(1);

- BEGIN

- << outer_loop >>

- FOR i IN 1..3 LOOP

- << inner_loop >>

- FOR j IN 1..3 LOOP

- dbms_output.put_line('i is: '|| i || ' and j is: ' || j);

- END loop inner_loop;

- END loop outer_loop;

- END;

- /

When this piece of code is executed, you will see the following result:

- i is: 1 and j is: 1

- i is: 1 and j is: 2

- i is: 1 and j is: 3

- i is: 2 and j is: 1

- i is: 2 and j is: 2

- i is: 2 and j is: 3

- i is: 3 and j is: 1

- i is: 3 and j is: 2

- i is: 3 and j is: 3

PL/SQL procedure successfully completed.

**Loop Control Statements**

A loop control statement changes the execution of the code from it would normally be. As soon as execution has left a scope, all the automatic objects in the scope will be destroyed. The following control statements are supported by SQL:

- EXIT statement - This completes the loop and passes control to the statement right after END LOOP

- CONTINUE statement - This makes the loop skip over the rest of its body and makes it test its condition before it restarts

- GOTO statement - Gives control to a labeled statement but be aware that it isn't recommended for you to use a GOTO statement in the program you write

## Java

On occasion, you may find it necessary to repeatedly execute a particular block of code in Java. As a rule, all statements are executed in a sequence with the first statement in the function being executed first, followed by the others in turn. Java supports the following loops:

- **while loop** - Provided a given condition is true, this will repeat a single or multiple statements and will test the condition before the loop body is executed.

- **for loop** - Allows a statement sequence to be execute repeatedly and abbreviates the loop variable management code

- **do...while loop** - Similar to a while statement but will test out the condition at the end of the loop

## Loop Control Statements:

As in SQL. These also change the normal sequence of the execution. When the scope is left, all the automatic objects in it are destroyed. These are the control statements supported by Java:

- break statement – Stops the switch or loop statement and

then immediately transfers execution to the statement that directly follows it

- continue statement - Makes the loop skip the rest of the body ad retest condition before restarting

**Java Enhanced For Loop**

Again, this is relatively new in Java and is used to traverse through a collection of elements. The following example shows you how it is written:

- for(declaration : expression)

- {

- //Statements

- }

**Declaration** – this is the new declared block variable, which is a type that is compatible with all of the elements in the array that you are trying to access. The variable is in the for block and has a value that is the same as the current element in the array.

**Expression** – this is that evaluates to the array that you are going to loop through. It can be a method call that returns an array or it can be an array variable.

An example:

- public class Test {

- ```
  public static void main(String args[]){
  ```

- ```
  int [] numbers = {10, 20, 30, 40, 50};
  ```

- ```
  for(int x : numbers ){
  ```

- ```
  System.out.print( x );
  ```

- ```
  System.out.print(",");
  ```

- ```
  }
  ```

- ```
  System.out.print("\n");
  ```

- ```
  String [] names ={"James", "Larry", "Tom", "Lacy"};
  ```

- ```
  for( String name : names ) {
  ```

- ```
  System.out.print( name );
  ```

- ```
  System.out.print(",");
  ```

- ```
  }
  ```

- ```
  }
  ```

- ```
  }
  ```

Executing this would give the following result:

- 10,20,30,40,50,

- James,Larry,Tom,Lacy,

## C++

As with the other languages, you may want to repeat a code execution a number of times and the statements are executed in sequence. The following loops are supported by C++:

- **while loop** – this will repeat a single or group of statements so long as a given condition is true and will test the condition before it begins the execution

- **for loop** – will repeatedly execute a sequence of statements and abbreviates the loop variable management code

- **do...while loop** – similar to the while statement but will test the condition that is at the end of the body

- **nested loops** – using this, you can use more than one loop inside any do...while, for or while loop

**Loop Control Statements:**

These change the normal sequence of the execution in exactly he same way as Java and SQL. These are control statements that are supported by C++:

- break statement - This stops the switch or loop statement and pushes the execution to the statement that immediately follows

- continue statement - This one makes the loop skip the rest of the body and will retest condition before it restarts

- goto statement - Puts control to the labelled statement but it isn't advisable to use this statement

**The Infinite Loop:**

If a condition can never become false then the loop will become an infinite loop. Traditionally in C++, we use the for loop. It is easy to make an endless loop with this because you do not need any of the three expressions that make up the for loop, meaning you can leave the conditional expression empty:

- #include <iostream>

- using namespace std;

- int main ()

- {

- for( ; ; )

- {

- printf("This loop will run forever.\n");

- }

- return 0;

- }

When there is no conditional expression, it is automatically assumed that it is true. You can have an increment and initialization expression but most C++ programmers will use the construct for(;;) to signal that it is an infinite or endless loop. You can terminate infinite loops easily by pressing on CTRL+C on your keyboard.

## Numbers

All programming languages provide support for manipulating different types of numbers such as floating point numbers or simple whole integers. Languages such as C and Java categorize these numbers in several categories based on their nature. (TurtorialsPoint, 2017) In the section where we explained about data types, we had listed the core data types i.e. number, small number, long number and decimal number. These data types are known as **primitive data types** and can be used to build more data types, which are called as user-defined data types. We have also explained you about the various logical and mathematical operators, so we know how to add, subtract and divide numbers etc. (TurtorialsPoint, 2017)

C programming language

In the following table we have listed various useful built-in mathematical functions available in C programming language.

| | |
|---|---|
| double sin(double); | It takes an angle (as a double) and returns the sine. |
| double cos(double); | It takes an angle (as a double) and returns the cosine. |
| double tan(double); | It takes an angle (as a double) and returns the tangent. |
| double pow(double, double); | First is a number you wish to raise and the second is the power you wish to raise it to. |
| double log(double); | It takes a number and returns the natural log of that number. |
| double hypot(double, double); | In case you pass this function the length of two sides of a right triangle, this function will return the length of hypotenuse. |
| int abs(int); | It will return the absolute value of an integer that is passed to it. |
| double sqrt(double); | When you pass this function a number, it returns its square root. |

| double floor(double); | This function finds the integer which is less than or equal to the argument passed to it. |
|---|---|
| double fabs(double); | It returns the absolute value of any decimal number passed to it. |

(TurtorialsPoint, 2017)

In order to use these functions you need to use math header file <math.h> in the same way as you use <stdio.h>

Java – numbers

Java provides almost all numeric data types that are available in C programming language. We use primitive data types such as double, byte, long, int etc. However, we can come across situations where we may need to use objects instead of primitive data types. Java provides wrapper classes in order to achieve this.

All wrapper classes such as; long, byte, double, integer, short, float are subclasses of the abstract class number. The object of the wrapper class wraps or contains its respective primitive data type. Compiler takes care of converting primitive data types into object, and it is called as **boxing**. Therefore, while using the wrapper class you just need to pass the value of the primitive data type to the constructor of the wrapper class. The wrapper object is will be then converted back to a primitive data type and this process is called as **unboxing**. (TurtorialsPoint, 2017)

Number methods in Java-

| | |
|---|---|
| compareTo( ) | It compares *this* object to the argument |
| xxxValue( ) | It converts the value of *this* number object to the xxx data type and returns it. |
| equals( ) | It determines whether *this* number object is equal to argument. |
| toString( ) | It returns a string object representing the value of a specified integer or int. |
| valueOf( ) | It returns an integer object holding the value of the specified primitive. |
| parseInt( ) | It is used to get the primitive data type of a certain string. |
| ceil( ) | It returns the smallest integer that is greater than or equal to the argument. It is returned as a double. |
| abs( ) | It returns the absolute value of the argument. |
| floor( ) | It returns the largest integer that is equal to or greater than the argument. It is returned as a double. |

| | |
|---|---|
| round( ) | It returns the closest int or long, as indicated by the method's return type to the argument. |
| rint( ) | It returns the integer that is closest in value to the argument. It is returned as a double. |
| min( ) | It returns the smaller of the two arguments. |
| exp( ) | It returns the base of the natural logarithms, e, to the power of argument. |
| max( ) | It returns larger of the two arguments. |
| log( ) | It returns the natural logarithm of the argument. |
| sqrt( ) | It returns the square root of the argument |
| pow( ) | It returns the value of first argument raise to the power of second argument. |
| cos( ) | It returns cosine of the specified double value |
| sin( ) | It returns the sine of the specified double value. |

| | |
|---|---|
| tan( ) | It returns tangent of the specified double value. |
| acos( ) | It returns the arccosine of the specified double value |
| asin( ) | It returns the arcsine of the specified double value. |
| atan( ) | It returns the arctangent of the specified double value. |
| atan2( ) | It converts rectangular coordinates (x,y) to polar coordinate (r, theta) and returns theta. |
| toRadians( ) | It converts the arguments to radians |
| toDegrees( ) | It converts the arguments to degrees |
| random( ) | It returns a random number. |

Numbers in SQL

SQL offers a variety of numeric data types to be used for different purposes –

1. Number – It is a true decimal data type that is ideal for working with monetary amounts. It is the only one of SQL's numeric data types to be implemented in a platform-independent fashion. It is the most common data type in SQL and is used to store integer, fixed point or floating-point

numbers of any size.

2. SIMPLE_INTEGER – This data type results in significantly shorter execution times for natively compiled code.

3. PLS_INTEGER - This integer data type conforming to your hardware's underlying integer representation. With your hardware's native machine instructions arithmetic is performed. You cannot store values of this type in tables, it is specific to SQL.

4. BINARY_FLOAT and BINARY_DOUBLE – These BINARY data types are highly specialized and are useful when you need to improve the performance of computation-intensive operations

## Characters

In computer programming, any single digit number like 0, 1, 2 and special characters like %, $, =, +, and so on are also treated as characters. In order to assign them in a character type variable you simply have to put them inside single quotes.

A character data type consumes 8 bits of memory that means that you can store anything in character that's ASCII value lies in between -127 to 127. A character data type can store any of the characters available on your keyboard including special characters like @, !, ^, $, %, *, &, (,), _, +, {,}, etc. Important point to remember here is that you can only keep a single alphabet or a single digit number inside single quotes.

Many programming languages support **Escape Sequence.** This means when a character is preceded by a backslash (\) and it has a special meaning to the compiler; it is called as Escape Sequence.

Following are the escape sequences available in C programming language –

| | |
|---|---|
| \b | it inserts a backspace in the text at this point. |
| \t | It inserts a tab in the text at this point |
| \n | It inserts a new line in the text at this point. |
| \f | It inserts a form feed in the text at this point |
| \r | It inserts a carriage return in the text at this point. |
| \' | It inserts a single quote character in the text. |
| \" | It inserts a double quote character in the text. |
| \\ | It inserts a backslash character in text. |

Characters in Java

The character data types are handled in similar fashion in Java as in C language. The Escape sequences are also the same as in C programming language (refer the table above). However, Java provides additional support for character manipulation.

Character methods in Java

| | |
|---|---|
| isDigit( ) | It determines whether the specified char value is a digit. |
| isLetter( ) | It determines whether the specified character value is a letter. |
| isWhitespace( ) | It determines whether the specified char value is white space. |
| isLowercase( ) | It determines whether the specified character is lowercase. |
| isUppercase( ) | It determines whether the specified character is uppercase. |
| toLowercase( ) | It returns the lowercase form if the specified character value. |
| toUppercase( ) | It returns the uppercase form of the specified character value. |
| toString( ) | It returns a String object representing the specified character value i.e. a one character string |

| character varying(n), varchar(n) | Variable-length with limit |
|---|---|
| character(n), char(n) | Fixed-length |
| text | Variable unlimited length |

The two primary character types in SQL are *varying(n)* and *character(n)*. Here, n is the positive integer. Both these types can store strings up to *n* characters in length. If you attempt to store a longer string into a column in any of these, it will result in an error, unless the excess characters are all spaces, and if this is the case then the string will be truncated to maximum length. If the string to be stored is shorter than the declared length, values of type *character* will be space-padded; values of type character *varying* will simply store the shorter string. (Ringer, 2016)

SQL recognizes the following 'special character' escape sequences –

| | |
|---|---|
| \0 | An ASCII NUL (X'00') character |
| \" | A double quote character |
| \' | A single quote character |
| \n | A newline character or linefeed character |
| \b | A backspace character |
| \r | A carriage return character |
| \Z | ASCII 26 (Control + Z) |
| \t | A tab character |
| \\ | A backslash character |
| \_ | A _ character |
| \% | A % character |

The \ _ and \ % sequences are used to search for literal instances of _ and % in pattern-matching contexts where otherwise they would be interpreted as wildcard characters.

A wildcard character is a character that can be used to substitute for any other character(s) in a string. Wildcard characters in SQL are as follows –

% - a substitute for zero or more characters

_ - a substitute for single character

[charlist] – Sets and ranges of characters to match

[^charlist] or [!charlist] – matches only a character NOT specified within the brackets. (SQL Wildcards)

# Java Arrays

An array is a data structure that stores a sequence of fixed size elements that are all the same size. In layman's terms, it is a storage place for a collection of data but is better thought of as a collection of variables that are all the same type.

In Java, instead of declaring the individual variables, like number0, number1, etc., we declare a single array variable, perhaps numbers, and then use number0, number1, etc. as a representation for the individual variables.

## Declaring Array Variables

If you want to use an array in your program, you have to declare a variable that will reference the array and you must also specify the array type that the variable is able to reference. This is the syntax you would use:

- dataType[] arrayRefVar;  //

Or

- dataType arrayRefVar[];  //

The top version is the preferred way. The following are examples of code showing the syntax:

- double[] myList;     //

Or

- double myList[];     //

**Creating Arrays:**

To create an array, you can use the new operator with this syntax:

- arrayRefVar = new dataType[arraySize];

This statement does two things:

- First, it creates the array using new dataType[arraySize];

- Second, the reference for the newly create array is given to the variable arrayRefVar

You can do all of this – declare an array variable, create an array and assign the reference to the variable in one single statement, as such:

- dataType[] arrayRefVar = new dataType[arraySize];

Or you can do this:

- dataType[] arrayRefVar = {value0, value1, ..., valuek};

The array elements can be accessed via the index. All array indices are 0-based which means that they begin from 0 to arrayRefVar.length-1. An example of this:

The following statement declares the array variable, creates the array containing 10 elements, each of double type, and then assigns the reference:

- double[] myList = new double[10];

**Processing Arrays:**

When we process the elements of an array we tend to use the for loop or the foreach loop, simply because all of those elements are the same types and we know what the array size is.

The following is an example that shows you how to create an array, followed by initialization and processing:

- public class TestArray {

- public static void main(String[] args) {

- double[] myList = {1.9, 2.9, 3.4, 3.5};

- // Print all the array elements

- for (int i = 0; i < myList.length; i++) {

- System.out.println(myList[i] + " ");

- }

- // Summing all elements

- double total = 0;

- for (int i = 0; i < myList.length; i++) {

```
    • total += myList[i];

    • }

    • System.out.println("Total is " + total);

    • // Finding the largest element

    • double max = myList[0];

    • for (int i = 1; i < myList.length; i++) {

    • if (myList[i] > max) max = myList[i];

    • }

    • System.out.println("Max is " + max);

    • }

    • }
```

Executing this code would give this result:

- 1.9

- 2.9

- 3.4

- 3.5

- Total is 11.7

- ax is 3.5

**The foreach Loops:**

Foreach lops were introduced in the Java Development Kit v 1.5 and they allow you to go through an entire array in sequence without the need to use an index variable.

The following example shows an array called myList and all the elements included in it:

- public class TestArray {

- public static void main(String[] args) {

- double[] myList = {1.9, 2.9, 3.4, 3.5};

- // Print all the array elements

- for (double element: myList) {

- System.out.println(element);

- }

- }

- }

Execution of this code would give this result:

- 1.9

- 2.9

- 3.4

- 3.5

**Passing Arrays to Methods:**
In the same way that you pass a primitive value to a method, you can also pass an array to a method. The following example shows the elements that are in an int array:

- public static void printArray(int[] array) {

- for (int i = 0; i < array.length; i++) {

- System.out.print(array[i] + " ");

- }

- }

We invoke this by passing the array. This example shows a statement that invokes a printArray method with the result of displaying 3, 1, 2, 6, 4, 2:

- printArray(new int[]{3, 1, 2, 6, 4, 2});

**Returning an Array from a Method:**
It is also possible for methods to return arrays. This example shows a method that returns an array that is actually the reverse of a different array:

- public static int[] reverse(int[] list) {

*186*

- int[] result = new int[list.length];

- for (int i = 0, j = result.length - 1; i < list.length; i++, j--) {

- result[j] = list[i];

- }

- return result;

- }

## The Arrays Class:

Included in the jave.util.arrays class, there are a number of static methods that allow you to search, sort, compare and fill any array element:

- **public static int binarySearch(Object[] a, Object key)** - Allows you to search a specified object array for a specified value by using the binary search algorithm. Before this call is made, the array must be sorted. The result will be the index of the search key provided it is in the list already.

- **public static boolean equals(long[] a, long[] a2)** - This will return true if the specified arrays of two longs are the same as each other. Arrays are considered to be equal if each contains the same amount of elements and all the corresponding element pairs in the arrays are equal.

- **public static void fill(int[] a, int val)** - This assigns the int value that is specified to each separate element of the array of ints specified.

- **public static void sort(Object[] a)** - This allows you to sort the objects of a specified array into ascending order.

# SQL

In SQL, we get a data structure that is called VARRAY and this can store a collection of fixed size sequential elements that are all the same type. Every VARRAY has contiguous memory locations, which means that the lowest address will correspond to the first element and the highest to the last. Each separate element in a VARRAY has an associated index and a maximum size that can be dynamically changed.

## Creating a VARRAY Type

VARRAY types are created using the CREATE TYPE statement. You need to specify the element types that will be stored in the array and the maximum size. To create a VARRAY type at schema level, the basic syntax should be:

- CREATE OR REPLACE TYPE varray_type_name IS VARRAY(n) of <element_type>

Where,

- varray_type_name is a valid attribute name,

- n is the number of elements (maximum) in the varray,

- element_type is the data type of the elements of the array.

To change the maximum size, you can use the ALTER TYPE statement, as such:

- CREATE Or REPLACE TYPE namearray AS VARRAY(3) OF VARCHAR2(10);

- /

- Type created.

To create a VARRAY type in an SQL block, you would use this basic syntax:

- TYPE varray_type_name IS VARRAY(n) of <element_type>

An example of that is:

- TYPE namearray IS VARRAY(5) OF VARCHAR2(10);

- Type grades IS VARRAY(5) OF INTEGER;

This example shows how to use VARRAYS:

- DECLARE

- type namesarray IS VARRAY(5) OF VARCHAR2(10);

- type grades IS VARRAY(5) OF INTEGER;

- names namesarray;

- marks grades;

- total integer;

- BEGIN

- names := namesarray('Kavita', 'Pritam', 'Ayan', 'Rishav', 'Aziz');

- marks:= grades(98, 97, 78, 87, 92);

- total := names.count;

- dbms_output.put_line('Total '|| total || ' Students');

- FOR i in 1 .. total LOOP

- dbms_output.put_line('Student: ' || names(i) || '

- Marks: ' || marks(i));

- END LOOP;

- END;

- /

Execution of this code is done at the SQL prompt and it will give this result:

- Student: Kavita  Marks: 98

- Student: Pritam  Marks: 97

- Student: Ayan  Marks: 78

- Student: Rishav  Marks: 87

- Student: Aziz  Marks: 92

- PL/SQL procedure successfully completed.

**Points to note:**

- In the Oracle environment, the beginning index for a VARRAY is always 1

- You can use the constructor method to initialize the elements in a VARRAY type so long as it has the same name as the VARRAY does

- VARRAYS are always one-dimensional

- VARRAYS are NULL when they are declared – before the elements can be referenced it must be initialized

In this example, we see the concept of a VARRAY being a %ROWTYPE of a database table or %TYPE of a database table field:

Select * from customers;

```
+----+----------+-----+-----------+----------+----------+----------+---------+
```

| ID | NAME       | AGE       | ADDRESS   |

SALARY   |

```
+----+----------+-----+-----------+----------+----------+---------+---
------+
```

| 1 | Ramesh         | 32|                Ahmedabad         |
2000.00 |

| 2 | Khilan         | 25 |               Delhi              |
1500.00 |

| 3 | kaushik        | 23 |               Kota               |
2000.00 |

| 4 | Chaitali       | 25 |               Mumbai             |
6500.00 |

| 5 | Hardik         | 27 |               Bhopal             |
8500.00 |

| 6 | Komal          | 22 |               MP                 |
4500.00 |

```
+----+----------+-----+-----------+----------+----------+----------+--
-------+
```

This example uses cursor:

- DECLARE

- CURSOR c_customers is

- SELECT name FROM customers;

- type c_list is varray (6) of customers.name%type;

- name_list c_list := c_list();

- counter integer :=0;

- BEGIN

- FOR n IN c_customers LOOP

- counter := counter + 1;

- name_list.extend;

- name_list(counter) := n.name;

- dbms_output.put_line('Customer('||counter ||'):'||name_list(counter));

- END LOOP;

- END;

- /

When we execute this code, we get this result:

- Customer(1): Ramesh

- Customer(2): Khilan

- Customer(3): kaushik

- Customer(4): Chaitali

- Customer(5): Hardik

- Customer(6): Komal

- PL/SQL procedure successfully completed.

# C++

C++ is similar to Java in the data structure of the array, storing sequential fixed size collection of elements. And, it is the same as SQL in that all arrays have contiguous memory locations

**Declaring Arrays:**

In C++, you must specify the element types and the number of elements that are required in the array:

- type arrayName [ arraySize ];

This a one-dimension array. The arraySize has to be an integer constant that is more than zero ad the type is any C++ data type, so long as it is valid. For example, if you wanted to declare an array with 10 elements, that is called a balance of type double, you would use this statement:

- double balance[10];

**Initializing Arrays:**

In C++, we initialize array elements in two ways – one at a time or by using one statement:

- double balance[5] = {1000.0, 2.0, 3.4, 17.0, 50.0};

The values between { } cannot be any bigger in number than the number of the elements that are declared between [ ]. This example shows you how to assign one ingle element of the array. Note that if you leave out the array size, an array that is just large enough to hold the initialization is created. So, if you were to write:

- double balance[] = {1000.0, 2.0, 3.4, 17.0, 50.0};

You are creating the same array that you did in the initial example:

- balance[4] = 50.0;

This statement assigns the element number that is fifth in the array with a value of 50.0. So, because arrays begin with 0 as the first element index, an array that has a 4th index will be numbered 5th.

### Accessing Array Elements:

Elements of an array can be accessed through indexing the name of the array. We do this by putting the element index inside square brackets following the array name. An example of that:

- double salary = balance[9];

This statement takes element 10 out of the array and gives the value to salary variable. The following example shows all of the above concepts – declaring, assigning and accessing the arrays:

- #include <iostream>

- using namespace std;

- #include <iomanip>

- using std::setw;

- int main ()

- {

- int n[ 10 ]; // n is an array of 10 integers

- // initialize elements of array n to 0

- for ( int i = 0; i < 10; i++ )

- {

- n[ i ] = i + 100; // set element at location i to i + 100

- }

- cout << "Element" << setw( 13 ) << "Value" << endl;

- // output each array element's value

- for ( int j = 0; j < 10; j++ )

- {

- cout << setw( 7 )<< j << setw( 13 ) << n[ j ] << endl;

- }

- return 0;

- }

When we compile and execute this code, we get this result:

| Element | Value |
|---------|-------|
| 0       | 100   |
| 1       | 101   |
| 2       | 102   |
| 3       | 103   |
| 4       | 104   |
| 5       | 105   |
| 6       | 106   |
| 7       | 107   |
| 8       | 108   |
| 9       | 109   |

# Strings

## Java

Strings are used a lot in Java and they are objects that contain a sequence of characters. Java allows users to both create and manipulate a string.

## Creating a String

The easiest way to create a string is this way:

- String greeting = "Hello world!";

Whenever the Java compiler comes across a string literal written in your code, it will create a string object; in the case of the syntax above it would be "Hello, World!".

In the same way you can with any object, you can use a constructor and the new keyword to create string objects. The string class in Java has 11 constructors in it, which enable you to use different sources to give the initial string value:

- public class StringDemo{

- public static void main(String args[]){

- char[] helloArray = { 'h', 'e', 'l', 'l', 'o', '.'};

- String helloString = new String(helloArray);

- System.out.println( helloString );

- }

- }

Compiling and executing this code would give this result:

- hello.

Be aware that the string class is immutable. This means that, once you have created the string object, you can't change it. If you find that you have to make changes to character strings then you should use the string builder and the string buffer classes.

**String Length:**

A method that is used to get information about a particular object is called an accessor. You can use the length() accessor method with strings, allowing you to return the value of the number of characters that are in the string object.

Below is an example of this method:

- public class StringDemo {

- public static void main(String args[]) {

- String palindrome = "Dot saw I was Tod";

- int len = palindrome.length();

- System.out.println( "String Length is : " + len );

- }

- }

- Which would give this result:

- String Length is : 17

**Concatenating Strings:**
There is also a method in the string class for concatenating two strings:

- string1.concat(string2);

This would return a new string, with string1 and the beginning and string 2 added to the end. You can also use this concat() method with string literals, as in this example:

- "My name is ".concat("Zara");

More commonly, we see strings concatenated with the + operator:

- "Hello," + " world" + "!"

-

And that gives this result:

- "Hello, world!"

-

Have a look at this example:

- public class StringDemo {

- public static void main(String args[]) {

- String string1 = "saw I was ";

- System.out.println("Dot " + string1 + "Tod");

- }

- }

Which would give this result:

- Dot saw I was Tod

**Creating Format Strings:**

You have two methods to print an output with formatted numbers – printf() and format(). In Java, the string class contains a class method that will return a string object instead of a printStream object – format(). This is a static method and using this lets you create a reusable formatted string instead of a one-time only print statement. As an example, instead of writing this:

- System.out.printf("The value of the float variable is " +

- "%f, while the value of the integer " +

- "variable is %d, and the string " +

- "is %s", floatVar, intVar, stringVar);

You can do this:

- String fs;

- fs = String.format("The value of the float variable is " +

- "%f, while the value of the integer " +

- "variable is %d, and the string " +

- "is %s", floatVar, intVar, stringVar);

- System.out.println(fs);

**String Methods:**
These are the methods that are supported by the string class in Java:

- **char charAt(int index)** - Will return the character at a specified index

- **int compareTo(Object o)** - Compares the specified string to another object

- **int compareTo(String anotherString)** - compares a pair of strings lexicographically

- **int compareToIgnoreCase(String str)** - compares a pair of strings lexicographically but ignoring any differences in case

- **String concat(String str)** - Concatenates the string that is specified to the end of the given string

- **boolean contentEquals(StringBuffer sb)** - Will return true if, and only if, the string has the same character sequence as the StringBuffer that is specified

- **static String copyValueOf(char[] data)** - Will return a string that shows the sequence of characters in the specified array

- **static String copyValueOf(char[] data, int offset, int count)** - Will return a string that shows the sequence of characters in the specified array

- **boolean endsWith(String suffix)** - Will test that the string finishes with the suffix that is specified

- **boolean equals(Object anObject)** - Will compare the string to the object that is specified

- **boolean equalsIgnoreCase(String anotherString)** - Will compare the string to another one but will ignore case

- **byte getBytes()** - Will encode the string to a byte sequence and uses the charset that is named. The result is stored in a new byte array

- **byte[] getBytes(String charsetName** - Does the same as the above method

- **void getChars(int srcBegin, int srcEnd, char[] dst, int dstBegin)** - Will copy specified characters from the string into the specified character array

- **int hashCode()** - Will return a hashcode for the particular string

- **int indexOf(int ch)** - Will return the index that is in this string of the first instance of the character specified

- **int indexOf(int ch, int fromIndex)** - Same as the above method but beginning the search at the index specified

- **int indexOf(String str)** - As above but from the first instance of the substring specified

- **int indexOf(String str, int fromIndex)** - As above but starting from the index that is specified

- **String intern()** - Will return a canonical representation for the specified string object

- **int lastIndexOf(int ch)** - Will return the index that is in the string, from the last instance of the character specified

- **int lastIndexOf(int ch, int fromIndex)** - As above but searches backwards, from the index specified

- **int lastIndexOf(String str)** - as above but returns the index that is the rightmost instant of the substring specified

- **int lastIndexOf(String str, int fromIndex)** - Will return the index in the string of the last instant of the substring specified, but searches backwards from the index specified

- **int length()** - will return the string length

- **boolean matches(String regex)** - will tell you if this string matches the regular expression that is given

- boolean regionMatches(boolean ignoreCase, int toffset, String other, int ooffset, int len) - Will test if two strings are equal to one another

- boolean regionMatches(int toffset, String other, int ooffset, int len) - Will test if two string regions ae equal to one another

- **String replace(char oldChar, char newChar)** - Will return a new string that is the result of the replacement of all the instants of oldChar with newChar

- **String replaceAll(String regex, String replacement** - Will replace all the substrings of the string that match up to the regular expression with the specified replacement

- String replaceFirst(String regex, String replacement) - As above but only replaces the first substring

- **String[] split(String regex)** - Will split the string around any matches of the specified regular expression

- String[] split(String regex, int limit) - As above

- **boolean startsWith(String prefix)** - Tests to see if the string begins with the prefix that is specified

- boolean startsWith(String prefix, int toffset) - As above but on a specified index

- **CharSequence subSequence(int beginIndex, int endIndex)** - Will return a new sequence of characters that is as a subsequence of the given sequence

- **String substring(int beginIndex)** - Will return a new string that will be a substring of the given string

- String substring(int beginIndex, int endIndex) - As above

- **char[] toCharArray()** - Will convert the string to a new character array

- **String toLowerCase()** - Will convert all characters in the string to lower case with the use of the rules for the given locale

- String toLowerCase(Locale locale) - As above

- **String toString()** - The object, a string, returns itself

- **String toUpperCase()** - Converts the characters int eh string to upper case, using the default locale rules

- **String toUpperCase(Locale locale)** - As above but using the given locale

- **String trim()** - Will return a copy of the string but omitting the leading and the trailing whitespaces

- **static String valueOf(primitive data type x)** - Will return the string representation of the specified data type argument

# C++

C++ has support for two string representations:

- C-style character string.

- String class type that was introduced along with standard C++

**The C-Style Character String:**

This came with the original C language and has been given full support in C++. It is a one-dimensional character array, terminated by a null character. The following example is of a declaration and initialization that creates a string with the word "Hello" in it. In order for the null character to be held at the end, the character array size must be one more than the amount of characters in the word "Hello":

- char greeting[6] = {'H', 'e', 'l', 'l', 'o', '\0'};

If you were to follow the array initialization rule, you could write that statement as this:

- char greeting[] = "Hello";

You do not actually put the null character on the end of the string constant because, when it initializes the array the compiler will place it at the end of the string for you.

The following example shows you how to print that string:

- #include <iostream>

- using namespace std;

- int main ()

- {

- char greeting[6] = {'H', 'e', 'l', 'l', 'o', '\0'};

- cout << "Greeting message: ";

- cout << greeting << endl;

- return 0;

- }

When we compile and execute this piece of code, we get this result:

- Greeting message: Hello

C++ provides support for a number of functions that are able to manipulate strings that are null-terminated:

- strcpy(s1, s2); - will copy string s2 to string s1

- strcat(s1, s2); - Will concatenate string s2 to the end of string s1

- strlen(s1); - Will return the length of the specified string

- strcmp(s1, s2); - Will return 0 provided s1 and s2 are identical and will return less than 0 if s1 is less than s2, greater than 0 if s1 is greater than s2.

- strchr(s1, ch); - Will return a pointer to the first instance of the specified character, ch, in string s1

- strstr(s1, s2); - will return a pointer to the first instance of string s2 in string s1

The following example shows some of these functions in use:

- #include <iostream>

- #include <cstring>

- using namespace std;

- int main ()

- {

- char str1[10] = "Hello";

- char str2[10] = "World";

- char str3[10];

- int  len ;

- // copy str1 into str3

- strcpy( str3, str1);

- cout << "strcpy( str3, str1) : " << str3 << endl;

- // concatenates str1 and str2

- strcat( str1, str2);

- cout << "strcat( str1, str2): " << str1 << endl;

- // total length of str1 after concatenation

- len = strlen(str1);

- cout << "strlen(str1) : " << len << endl;

- return 0;

- }

- When we compile and execute this code, we get a result like this one:

- strcpy( str3, str1) : Hello

- strcat( str1, str2): HelloWorld

- strlen(str1) : 10

## The String Class in C++:

This string class supports all of those functions that we mentioned above as well as many more besides. The following example uses objects and classes:

- #include <iostream>

- #include <string>

- using namespace std;

- int main ()

- {

- string str1 = "Hello";

- string str2 = "World";

- string str3;

- int len ;

- // copy str1 into str3

- str3 = str1;

- cout << "str3 : " << str3 << endl;

- // concatenates str1 and str2

- str3 = str1 + str2;

- cout << "str1 + str2 : " << str3 << endl;

- // total length of str3 after concatenation

- len = str3.size();

- cout << "str3.size() : " << len << endl;

- return 0;

- }

When compiled and executed, the above code produces this result:

- str3 : Hello

- str1 + str2 : HelloWorld

- str3.size() : 10

## SQL

SQL strings are character sequences with an optional specification of size. These characters can be alpha, numeric, special characters, blank spaces, or a combination of all of these. SQL supports three string types:

- **Fixed Length** - You specify how long the string is while declaring it. Strings are right-padded with spaces that correspond to the specified length

- **Variable Length** - Can be a maximum length of 32,767 characters and there is no padding

- **CLOBs – Character Large Objects** - Variable in length up to 128 terabytes in size

SQL strings can be literal or they can be variable. String literals must be enclosed inside quotation marks, as such:

- 'This is a string literal.' Or 'hello world'

If you want to include a single quote in a string literal, you must use a pair of single quotes beside each other:

- 'this isn''t what it looks like'

**Declaring String Variables**
There are quite a number of string datatypes in the Oracle database, including NVARCHAR, VARCHAR2, CHAR, CHAR, CLOB and NCLOB. Those that have an N as a prefix are "national character types" and will store character data in Unicode.

If you have to declare a string that is variable length, you have to provide the maximum string length. This example demonstrates the declaration and use of some of the string variables:

```
DECLARE
name varchar2(20);
company varchar2(30);
introduction clob;
choice char(1);
BEGIN
name := 'John Smith';
company := 'Infotech';
introduction := ' Hello! I''m John Smith from Infotech.';
choice := 'y';
IF choice = 'y' THEN
dbms_output.put_line(name);
dbms_output.put_line(company);
dbms_output.put_line(introduction);
END IF;
END;
/
```

When we compile and execute this code, we get this result:

- John Smith

- Infotech Corporation

- Hello! I'm John Smith from Infotech.

- PL/SQL procedure successfully completed

You would use the CHAR datatype to declare a fixed length string and you do not need to specify the maximum length. If you omit the length constraint, Oracle will automatically use the maximum length that is required. These two examples are actually the same:

- red_flag CHAR(1) := 'Y';

- red_flag CHAR   := 'Y';

## SQL String Functions and Operators

SQL uses the concatenation operator to join two strings together - (||). Below are the SQL string functions.

- **ASCII(x);** - Will return the ASCII value of the specified character

- **CHR(x);** - Will return the character with the specified ASCII value

- **CONCAT(x, y);** - will concatenate the two specified strings and return the new string – one string with the other appended

- **INITCAP(x);** - Will convert the first letter of each word in the specified string to uppercase and then returns the new string

- **INSTR(x, find_string [, start] [, occurrence]);** - Will search for the specified string and return he position it finds it at

- **INSTRB(x);** - will return the location of the specified string inside another string but the result is the value in bytes

- **LENGTH(x);** - will return the number of characters in the specified string

- **LENGTHB(x);** - Will return the character string length in bytes for character sets that are single byte

- **LOWER(x);** - Will convert the letters in the specified string to lower case and then return the new string

- **LPAD(x, width [, pad_string]) ;** - Will pad the specified string with spaces on the left to make the total number of characters match the width characters

- **LTRIM(x [, trim_string]);** - Will trim off the characters to the left of the specified string

- **NANVL(x, value);** - Will return the value provided x is the same as the NaN special value. If not an x is returned

- **NLS_INITCAP(x);** - This is the same as INITCAP function but uses a different method of sorting

- **NLS_LOWER(x) ;** - This is the same as the LOWER function with a different sort method

- **NLS_UPPER(x);** - This is the same as the UPPER function with a different sort method

- **NLSSORT(x);** - This changes the method used to sort the characters and must be specified before NLS functions. If not, the default sort method is used

- **NVL(x, value);** - Will return a value if x is a null. If not then x will be returned

- **NVL2(x, value1, value2);** - will return value1 if x is not a null but, if it is, it will return value2

- **REPLACE(x, search_string, replace_string);** - Will search the specified string and replace it with the specified text

- RPAD(x, width [, pad_string]); - Will pad x on the right

- **RTRIM(x [, trim_string]);** - Will trim x from the right

- **SOUNDEX(x) ;** - Will return a string that contains the

phonetic representation

- **SUBSTR(x, start [, length]);** - Will return a substring that starts at the specified position. You can supply an length for the substring if you wish but this is optional

- **SUBSTRB(x);** - This is the same as SUBSTR except for the parameter expression n bytes instead of in characters where the character system is single byte

- **TRIM([trim_char FROM) x);** - Will trim the characters from both left and right

- **UPPER(x);** - Will convert the letters to uppercase and then return the new string

Below are some examples that show these functions in use.

**Example 1**

- DECLARE

- greetings varchar2(11) := 'hello world';

- BEGIN

- dbms_output.put_line(UPPER(greetings));

- dbms_output.put_line(LOWER(greetings));

- dbms_output.put_line(INITCAP(greetings));

- /* retrieve the first character in the string */

- dbms_output.put_line ( SUBSTR (greetings, 1, 1));

- /* retrieve the last character in the string */

- dbms_output.put_line ( SUBSTR (greetings, -1, 1));

- /* retrieve five characters,

- starting from the seventh position. */

- dbms_output.put_line ( SUBSTR (greetings, 7, 5));

- /* retrieve the remainder of the string,

- starting from the second position. */

- dbms_output.put_line ( SUBSTR (greetings, 2));

- /* find the location of the first "e" */

- dbms_output.put_line ( INSTR (greetings, 'e'));

- END;

- /

Execution of the above code results in this:

- HELLO WORLD

- hello world

- Hello World

- h

- d

- World

- ello World

- 2

- PL/SQL procedure successfully completed.

## Example 2

- DECLARE

- greetings varchar2(30) := '......Hello World.....';

- BEGIN

- dbms_output.put_line(RTRIM(greetings,'.'));

- dbms_output.put_line(LTRIM(greetings, '.'));

- dbms_output.put_line(TRIM( '.' from greetings));

- END;

- /

- And the result of this code is this:

- ......Hello World

- Hello World.....

- Hello World

- PL/SQL procedure successfully completed.

**Defining a function in C programming**

The typical form of function definition in C language is –

return_type function_name( parameter list) {

body of the function

return [expression]

}

C programming language consists of a function header and a function body. All parts of a function are defined below –

- Return Type –The return_type is the data type of the value the function returns. Without returning a value, some functions perform the desired operations.

- Function Name – The function parameter list and function name together constitute the function signature.

- Parameter List – You pass a value as a parameter when a function is invoked. This value is referred to as the actual argument or parameter. The parameter list refers to the order, type and number of parameters of a function. A function may not contain a parameter, since parameters are optional.

- Function body – It contains a collection of statements that defines what the function does.

- (TurtorialsPoint, 2017)

How to call a function in C programming?

For creating a C function, you will have to give a definition of what the function has to do. In order to use the function, call that function to perform a defined task.

## Functions in C++

The function definition is same as in C programming language.

Function declarations – This tells the compiler about how to call a function and a function name. The actual body of the function can be defined separately. Function declaration has the following parts –

return_type function_name( parameter list);

Parameters names are not important in function declaration only their type is required. When you define a function in one source file and you call that function in another file then the function declaration is required. In such a case, you should declare the function at the top of the file calling the function. (Tandukar, 2014)

## How to call a function in C++?

In order to create a C++ function, you define what the function has to do and in order to use that function, you have to invoke or call that function. Program control is transferred to the called function when a program calls a function. A called function performs the defined task only when its return statement is executed or when its function-ending closing brace is reached. It returns program control back to the main program. In order to call a function, you just need to pass the required parameters along with function name and if function returns a value, then you can store returned value.

(Arora, 2014)

## Function Arguments

To use arguments in a function, it must declare variables that accept the values of arguments and these variables are known as **formal parameters** of a function. These parameters behave like other local variables inside the function and created upon entry into the function and destroyed upon exit. There are three ways that arguments can be passed to a function, while you call a function, they are –

- Call by Value - In this method, the actual value of an argument is copied into formal parameter of the function. Here, changes made to parameter inside the function have no effect on the argument.

- Call by reference – In this method, the reference of an argument is copied into the formal parameter. The reference is used inside the function to access the actual argument used in call which means that changes made to the parameter affect the argument.

- Call by pointer- In this method, the address of the argument is copied into the formal parameter. The address is used inside the function to access the actual argument used in the call which means that changes made to the parameter affect the argument.  (Lavanya, 2015)

However, by default C++ uses call by value to pass arguments. Typically this means that code within a function cannot alter the arguments used to call the function.

(TurtorialsPoint, 2017)

Default Values for Parameters –
The default value for each of the last parameters can be specified when you define a function. If the corresponding argument is left blank when calling to a function, this value will be used. It is done by using the assignment operator and assigning values for the arguments in the function definition. When the function is called and the value for that parameter is not passed, the default given value is used. In case the value is specified, this default value is ignored and instead passed value is used.

(Lavanya, 2015)

## Creating methods in JAVA

Functions are called as methods in Java. It is a collection of statements that are grouped together to perform an operation.

How to create method in JAVA?

Let us look at the following example to understand the syntax of a method in JAVA –

public static int methodName(int a, int b) {

  // body

}

In the above example,

public static is the modifier

int is return_type

methodName is name of the method

a,b are formal parameters

int a, int b are list of parameters

The method definition consists of a method header and a body. Example –

modifier returnType nameofMethod (Parameter List) {

  // method body

}

The above syntax includes the following –

- Modifier - this defines the optional use of the method and its access type.

- returnType – method may return a value.

- nameOfMethod – the method signature consists of the method name and the parameter list. It is the name of the method.

- Parameter List - It is the list of parameters, it is the order, type and number of parameters of a method. They may contain zero parameters and are optional.

- method body – it defines what method does with the statements.

(TurtorialsPoint, 2017)

How to call a method?

In order to use a method it should be called and there are two ways to do this; first method returns a value or returns no value. Like C++, the process is simple when a method is invoked by a program, the program control gets transferred to the called method and this called method then returns control to the caller under the following two conditions –

- When the return statement is executed

- When it reaches the method ending closure brace.

Method returning void is considered as call to a statement.

Other important things to note in Java methods are –

- The void keyword – It allows you to create methods which do not return a value.

- Passing parameters by value – Arguments are to be passed while working under the calling process and they should be in the same order as their respective parameters in the method specification. The passing of parameters can be done by reference or value. Passing parameters by value means calling a method with a parameter and through this the argument value is passed to the parameter.

- Method overloading – This means when a class has more than two methods with same name but different parameters. Method overloading is different from overriding since in overriding, a method has the same type, method name and number of parameters.

- Using Command-Line Arguments – Sometimes when you run a program you may want to pass some information into it. This is done by command-line arguments to *main( )*. It is the information that directly follows the program's name on the command line when it is executed. Command-Line arguments are stored as strings in the String array passed to the *main( )* and are easily accessible.

- Constructors – It initializes an object when it is created and has the same name as its class. It is syntactically similar to a method and has no explicit return type. Generally, you will use constructors to give initial values to the instance variables defined by the class, or to carry out any start up procedures which are required to create a fully formed object. Whether you define or not, but all classes have constructors since Java automatically provides a default constructor that initializes all member variables to zero. But once you define your own constructor, then the default is not used any longer.

- Parameterized Constructors – Often you would need a constructor that accepts more than one parameter. The parameters are added to a constructor in the same way as they are added to a method; you just have to declare them inside the parentheses after the constructor's name.

- *this* keyword - In Java, the *this* keyword is used as a reference to the object of the current class, within an instance method or a constructor. By using this keyword you can refer the members of a class such as; variables, methods and constructors.

- Please note that *this* keyword is used only within instance constructors or methods.

- The *finalize( )* method – it is possible to define a method that can be called immediately before an object's final destruction by the garbage collector. It is called as the *finalize( )* method, and it can be used to ensure than an object is cleanly terminated.

(TurtorialsPoint, 2017)

## Creating functions in SQL

A standalone function is created using the CREATE FUNCTION statement. We have mentioned below a simple syntax for the CREATE or REPLACE PROCEDURE statement -

CREATE [OR REPLACE] FUNCTION function_name

[ ( parameter_name [IN | OUT | IN OUT] type [, . . .])]

RETURN return_datatype

{IS | AS}

BEGIN

    <function_body>

END [function_name];

In the above syntax,

- Function_name – it specifies the name of the function.

- [OR REPLACE] – This option allows modifying an existing function.

- The function must contain a **return** statement.

- The optional parameter list contains mode, name and types of the parameters. OUT represents that this parameter will be used to return a value outside of the procedure and IN represents that value will be passed from outside.

- RETURN clause specifies that data type you are going to return from the function.

- The *function_body* consists of the executable part.

- To create a standalone function the AS keyword is used instead of IS keyword.

(Java T Point)

How to call a function?

You have to give a definition of what function has to do while creating it. In order to use a function, you will have to call that function to carry out the defined task. A program control is transferred to the called function when a program calls a function. A defined task is performed by the called function when its return statement is executed or when its last end statement is reached. It returns program control back to the main program.

In order to call a function you simply need to pass the required parameters along with function name and if function returns value then you can store the returned value. (TurtorialsPoint, 2017)

SQL has many built-in functions for performing processes on numeric data or strings.

- SQL MAX Function – this aggregate function allows you to select the maximum value for a certain column.

- SQL COUNT Function – this function is used to count the number of rows in a database table.

- SQL MIN Function- this aggregate function allows you to select the minimum value for a certain column.

- SQL SUM Function – this function allows selecting the total for a numeric column.

- SQL AVG Function – this function selects the average value for certain table column.

- SQL SQRT Function – this function uses the SQL command to generate a square root of a given number.

- SQL RAND Function - this function uses the SQL command to generate a random number.

- SQL Numeric Function - To manipulate numbers in SQL, a complete list of SQL functions is required.

- SQL CONCAT Function – this function is used to concatenate any string inside any SQL command.

- SQL String Function - To manipulate strings in SQL, a complete list of SQL functions is required.

(TurtorialsPoint, 2017)

# Chapter 8
# File I/O in Computer Programming

<u>What are computer files?</u>

Computer file is used to store data in digital format like image, plain text, or any other content. These files can be organized inside different directories and are used to keep digital data, whereas directories are used to keep files. While you program, you can keep your source code in text files with different extensions. For example in JAVA you can save as **.java** and C programming files it can be saved with extension **.c**

<u>File Input/Output</u>

Typically, you create files using text editors such as MS word, MS excel, notepad or MS PowerPoint etc. We can also modify an existing file using a computer program. Input means data that is written into a file and output means that data which is read from the file.

<u>File operation modes</u>

Before you start working with any file using a computer program, either you will have to create a new file if it does not exist or open the already existing file. We can open a file in the following modes in either of the cases –

- Read-Only mode – If you do not want to write any further content in an existing file and just want to read it, then you will open the file in read-only mode. All programming languages provide syntax to open files in read-only mode.

- Write-Only mode – If you just want to write and not read the content in an existing file or a newly created file, then you will open the file in write-only mode. All programming languages provide syntax to open files in write-only mode.

- Read & Write Mode – In case you want to do both read and write in the same file then you open file in the read & write mode.

- Append Mode – When you open file for writing, it will allow you to write from the beginning of the file and if there is any existing content then it will overwrite it. Now if you don't want it to overwrite the existing content, then we open the file in append mode. All programming languages provide syntax to open files in append mode.

Opening Files

The *fopen( )* function is used to open an existing file or to create a new file. This call will initialize an object of the type FILE, which contains all the necessary information that is necessary to control the stream. Following is the signature of this function call *FILE \*fopen( const char \*filename, const char \* mode)*, where **filename** is the string literal, which is used to name your file and access mode can have can have one of the following values –

| | |
|---|---|
| r | for reading purpose it opens a text file |
| w | It opens a text file for writing. In case it does not exist, then a new file is created. In this case, your program will start writing content from beginning of the file. |
| a | It opens a text file for writing in appending mode. A new file is created in case it does not exist. In this case, your program will start appending content in the existing file content. |
| r+ | It opens a text file for both reading and writing purposes. |
| w+ | It opens a text file for both reading and writing purposes. First it truncates the file to zero length, in case it exists, otherwise creates the file in case it does not exist. |
| a+ | It opens at text file for both reading and writing purposes. A file is created in case it does not exist. Here, writing can only appended but reading will start from the beginning. |

(TurtorialsPoint, 2017)

## Closing a file

The *fclose( ) function is used to close a file.* The prototype of this function is as follows –

int fclose(FILE *fp);

The function *fclose( )* returns zero on success, or **EOF**( it is a constant defined in the header file *stdio.h*), special character in case there is an error in closing the file. It actually flushes the data that is still pending in the buffer to the file. It then closes the file, and releases any memory used for the file.

Various functions are provided by C standard library to read or write a file character by character or in the form of a fixed length string.

## Writing a file

The simplest function to write individual characters to a stream is as mentioned below –

int fputc( int c, FILE *fp)

In the above function, *fputc( )* writes the character value of the argument c to the output stream referenced by fp. On success it returns the written character written, otherwise EOF in case of an error. In order to write a null- terminated string to a stream, you can write the following function –

int fputs( const char * s, FILE *fp)

Here, *fputs( )* writes the string **s** into the file referenced by **fp**. On success it returns a non-negative value, otherwise EOF is returned in case any error occurs. To write a string to a file you can also use the function-

int fprint(FILE *fp,const char *format,...)

Reading a file

The simplest function to read a text file character by character is as mentioned below-

int fgetc( FILE * fp);

The function, *fgetc( )* reads a character from the input file referenced by **fp.** Return value is the character read and in case of any error it returns EOF. To read a string from a stream, you can use the following function –

char *fgets( char *buf, int n, FILE *fp);

Here, the function *fgets( )* reads upto n – 1 characters from the input stream referenced by **fp**. The read string is copied into the buffer **buf** and to terminate the string it appends the **null** character.

In case this function encounters a newline '\n' or EOF before they have read the maximum number of characters, then it returns only the characters read up to that point including the new line character. To read string from a file you can also use the function *int fscanf(FILE \*fp, const char\*format,...)*, but it will stop reading after encountering the first space character.

(TurtorialsPoint, 2017)

## JAVA

Java has set of functions to handle File I/O. A sequence of data in Java is called as stream. There are two types of streams –

- Input Stream – it is used to read data from source.

- Output Stream – it is used for writing data to a destination.

### Reading and Writing Files

The InputStream is used to read data from a source and the OutputStream is used for writing data to a destination. (YURI56, 2013)

FileInputStream – This stream is used for reading data from the files and objects can be created by using the keyword **new.**

FileOutputStream – This is used to create a file and write data into it. It will create a file in case there is no existing file before it opening it for output.

# Chapter 9
# Advanced Java

## Data Structures

The Java utility package provides a number of very powerful data structures that perform a range of different functions. These structures are made up of the following classes and interfaces:

- Enumeration

- BitSet

- Vector

- Stack

- Dictionary

- Hashtable

- Properties

## The Enumeration:

This interface is not actually a data structure but it holds great importance in the context of the other data structures. The interface for Enumeration defines a way of retrieving successive elements from within a data structure.

For example, Enumeration defines something called nextElement, a method that we use to get the next element from a data structure that has a number of elements.

### The BitSet

This class is used to implement a group of flags or bits that can be set and/or cleared on an individual basis. This is a useful lass to use when you need to be able to keep up with a set of Boolean value – all you do is assign a bit to each of the values and then set it or clear it as required.

### The Vector

This one is similar to the traditional Java array with one exception – it is able to grow as needed to accommodate more elements. Like the array, the elements of the Vector object are accessible through an index directly into the Vector.

The good thing about the Vector class s that there is no need to worry about setting a specific size for it when you create it – instead, it will grow and shrink as needed.

### The Stack

The Stack class is responsible for implementing a LIFO (Last In, First Out) element stack. Think of a stack as being a pile of objects, all stacked up vertically. When a new one is added, it goes on top of the stack.

When an element is pulled out of the stack, it too comes from the top. The last element to go on is the first one to come off.

## The Dictionary

This is an abstract class that will define a data structure for the mapping of keys to values. This is useful when you need to be able to get at data using a specific key, instead of using an integer index.

Because the Dictionary class is an abstract, it only gives you the framework for a data structure that has been key-mapped, rather than for a particular implementation.

## The Hashtable

This class gives us a means of organizing the data based on a key structure defined by the user. For example, if you have an address list hash table, you can store data and sort it based on a specific key, like a ZIP code, rather than using names.

The meaning of the keys in the hashtables is entirely dependent on what the hash table is used for and on the data contained in it.

## The Properties

This one is a subclass of the previous class, hashtables, and it is used for maintaining lists of values. In these values, the key is a String, as is the value. The Properties class is used by a number of other Java classes, i.e. it is the object type that is returned by System.getProperties() when getting environmental values.

## Collections Framework

Before Java-2, Java gave us a number of adohoc classes to use for the storage and manipulation of groups of objects; classes such as Dictionary, Stack, Vector and Properties. While these were useful classes, they didn't have a central theme, a unifying theme and, as such, the way that you used one of these classes is was not the same as you would use another. The Collections Framework was put into place to meet a number of important goals:

- It had to be of high performance and the implementations for the central collection, such as the dynamic array, trees, lined lists and hashtables, are very efficient.

- The framework needed to let different types of collections work in a manner that was similar to each other and to be able to interoperate to a high degree.

- It had to be made easy to extend and/or adapt a collection

To this end, the framework has been designed around a set of interfaces that have been standardized. There are a number of standard implementations of the interfaces that can be used as they are and you can also implement a collection of your own choosing. Some of toes standard implementations are HashSet, LinkedList and TreeSet.

A collection framework is an architecture that has been unified for the representation and manipulation of collections. Every framework has the following:

- **Interfaces:** These are abstract data types that are representative of collections. They allow each of the collections to be independently manipulated, outside of the details of representations. In any object-oriented language, interfaces will usually form a hierarchy.

- **Implementations, i.e., Classes:** These are solid implementations of each of the collection interfaces and are basically data structures that can be reused.

- **Algorithms:** Algorithms are methods used for performing computations that are useful, like searching and sorting, on any objet that may implement a collection interface. These algorithms are said to be "polymorphic", which means that one method can be used on a number of implementation of an appropriate collection interface.

As well as collections, the Framework also defines a number of different classes and map interfaces. Maps are used to store key and value pairs and, although they are not collections as such, they are integrated with them.

**The Collection Interfaces:**
A number of different interfaces are defined by the collections framework. The table below gives you a brief explanation of each interface:

| Interfaces with Description |
|---|
| **The Collection Interface**<br><br>This allows you to work with object groups and is the at the top of the hierarchy. |
| **The List Interface**<br><br>This extends the Collection interface and an instance of this one stores a collection of elements that are ordered. |
| **The Set**<br><br>This one extends Collection so that it can handle sets. These sets have to contain elements that are unique. |
| **The SortedSet**<br><br>This will extend Set so that it can handle sorted sets |
| **The Map**<br><br>This maps unique keys to values. |

| |
|---|
| **The Map.Entry**<br><br>This describes an element, or a key/value pair, in a map and is an inner class of Map |
| **The SortedMap**<br><br>This extends Map in order to allow the keys to be maintained in an ascending order. |
| **The Enumeration**<br><br>This is a legacy interface that defines methods that you can use to enumerate, or get one at a time, elements from a collection of objects. This has now been superseded by Iterator. |

## The Collection Classes:

As well as the collection interfaces, Java also provides us with a number of standard collection lasses, all of which are deigned to implement the interfaces to some degree or other. Some will provide full implementation that can be used as they are and others are more of an abstract class, a thinned down implementation that is used purely as a starting point for creating more solid collections. The following table is a summary of the standard collection classes.

| Classes with Description |
| --- |
| **AbstractCollection**<br><br>Will implement almost all of the collection interface |
| **AbstractList**<br><br>Will implement most of the List interface and also extends AbstractCollection |
| **AbstractSequentialList**<br><br>Will extend AbstractList so that a collection that uses sequential element ace, rather than random access can use it |
| **LinkedList**<br><br>Extends AbstractSequentialList to implement a linked list |
| **ArrayList**<br><br>Extends AbstractList so that a dynamic array can be implemented |

| | |
|---|---|
| **AbstractSet** | |
| Wil extend AbstractCollection and then implement almost all of the Set interface | |
| **HashSet** | |
| Will extend AbstractSet so it can be used with a hash table | |
| **LinkedHashSet** | |
| Will extend HashSet so that insertion-order iterations can be used | |
| **TreeSet** | |
| Will extend AbstractSet and also allows implementation of sets that are stored in trees | |
| **AbstractMap** | |
| Will implement almost all of the Map interface | |
| **HashMap** | |
| Will extend AbstractMap so it can use a hashtable | |

| | |
|---|---|
| **TreeMap** | |
| Will extend AbstractMap so it can use a tree | |
| **WeakHashMap** | |
| Will extend AbstractMap so it can use a hash table that contains weak keys | |
| **LinkedHashMap** | |
| Will extend HashMap so that insertion-order iterations can be used | |
| **IdentityHashMap** | |
| Will extend AbstractMap and will also use reference equality when it compares documents | |

The following classes only provide a basic, skeletal implementation of core interfaces so that the effort needed to implement them is reduced:

- AbstractCollection

- AbstractSet

- AbstractList

- AbstractMap

- AbstractSequentialList

## The Collection Algorithms:

The collections framework also defines a number of algorithms that may be applied to certain maps and collections. These are defined within the Collections class as static methods.

Some of these methods are able to throw a ClassCastException. This happens when an attempt is expected to try and compare incompatible types. These methods an also throw up UnsupportedOperationException when an attempt is made to try and modify a collection that cannot be modified.

Collections will define no less than three static variables, all of which are immutable:

- EMPTY_SET

- EMPTY_LIST

- EMPTY_MAP

The following table shows the methods that are defined within the Collection Algorithms:

| Methods with Description |
| --- |
| **static int binarySearch(List list, Object value, Comparator c)**<br><br>Will search for a value in a list that is ordered according to c. It will return the position of the value in the list or, if no value is found, it will return -1 |
| **static int binarySearch(List list, Object value)**<br><br>Will search for a value in a list which must be sorted. It will return the value position or -1 if none is found |
| **static void copy(List list1, List list2)**<br><br>Will copy the elements from list2 into list1 |
| **static Enumeration enumeration(Collection c)**<br><br>Will return an enumeration over c. |
| **static void fill(List list, Object obj)**<br><br>Will assign obj to each of the elements of a list |

## static int indexOfSubList(List list, List subList)

Will search for the first time that subList appears and will return the index or, if none found, will return .1

## static int lastIndexOfSubList(List list, List subList)

Will search for the final occurrence of subList in the list and return the index if found. If not, will return .1

## static ArrayList list(Enumeration enum)

Will return an Arraylist containing the elements of enum

## static Object max(Collection c, Comparator comp)

Will return the maximum element of c, determined by comp

## static Object max(Collection c)

Will return the maximum element of c, as determined by ordering; the collection does not need to be sorted first.

## static Object min(Collection c, Comparator comp)

Will return the minimum element of c, determined by comp. The collection doesn't need to be sorted first

| |
|---|
| **static Object min(Collection c)** |
| Will return the minimum element of c, determined by ordering |
| **static List nCopies(int num, Object obj)** |
| Will return num copies of obj that are contained within an immutable list. num has to be equal to or greater than zero |
| **static boolean replaceAll(List list, Object old, Object new)** |
| Will replace all instances of old with new in a specified list and will return true if one or more replacements happen. If none, false is returned |
| **static void reverse(List list)** |
| Will reverse the list sequence |
| **static Comparator reverseOrder( )** |
| Will return a reverse comparator |
| **static void rotate(List list, int n)** |
| Will rotate the list n places right. If you want to rotate left, you must be a negative n value |

### static void shuffle(List list)

Will shuffle all the list elements

### static Set singleton(Object obj)

Will return obj as an immutable set, a very easy way of converting one object to a set

### static List singletonList(Object obj)

Will return obj as an immutable list, an easy way of converting a single object to a pair

### static Map singletonMap(Object k, Object v)

Will return the key and value pair k/v as an immutable map, a very easy way of converting a single pair to a map.

### static void sort(List list, Comparator comp)

Will sort the list elements as determined by comp

### static void sort(List list)

Will sort the list element a per natural ordering

| |
|---|
| **static void swap(List list, int idx1, int idx2)** |
| Will exchange list elements at indies that are specified by idx1 and idx2 |
| **static Collection synchronizedCollection(Collection c)** |
| Will return a thread-safe collection that is backed by c |
| **static List synchronizedList(List list)** |
| will return a thread-safe list that is backed by list |
| **static Map synchronizedMap(Map m)** |
| will return a thread-safe Map that is backed by list m. |
| **static Set synchronizedSet(Set s)** |
| will return a thread-safe set that is backed by s. |
| **static SortedMap synchronizedSortedMap(SortedMap sm)** |
| will return a thread-safe sorted set that is backed by sm |
| **static SortedSet synchronizedSortedSet(SortedSet ss)** |
| Will return a thread-safe set that is backed by ss. |

| static Collection unmodifiableCollection(Collection c) |
|---|
| Will return an unmodifiable collection that is backed by c. |
| static List unmodifiableList(List list) |
| Will return an unmodifiable list that is backed by list. |
| static Map unmodifiableMap(Map m) |
| will return an unmodifiable map that is backed by m. |
| static Set unmodifiableSet(Set s) |
| will return an unmodifiable set that is backed by s. |
| static SortedMap unmodifiableSortedMap(SortedMap sm) |
| Will return an unmodifiable sorted map that is backed by sm. |
| static SortedSet unmodifiableSortedSet(SortedSet ss) |
| Will return an unmodifiable sorted set that is backed by ss. |

The following example code shows a number of algorithms in use:

- import java.util.*;

```java
public class AlgorithmsDemo {

public static void main(String args[]) {

// Create and initialize linked list

LinkedList ll = new LinkedList();

ll.add(new Integer(-8));

ll.add(new Integer(20));

ll.add(new Integer(-20));

ll.add(new Integer(8));

// Create a reverse order comparator

Comparator r = Collections.reverseOrder();

// Sort list by using the comparator

Collections.sort(ll, r);

// Get iterator

Iterator li = ll.iterator();

System.out.print("List sorted in reverse: ");

whilc(li.hasNext()){

System.out.print(li.next() + " ");
```

- }

- System.out.println();

- Collections.shuffle(ll);

- // display randomized list

- li = ll.iterator();

- System.out.print("List shuffled: ");

- while(li.hasNext()){

- System.out.print(li.next() + " ");

- }

- System.out.println();

- System.out.println("Minimum: " + Collections.min(ll));

- System.out.println("Maximum: " + Collections.max(ll));

- }

- }

Inputting this into your system would produce this result:

- List sorted in reverse: 20 8 -8 -20

- List shuffled: 20 -20 8 -8

- minimum: -20

- maximum: 20

## Java Iterator

In case you want to display each element in a collection, the easiest way to do is to employ an iterator. Iterator is an object that implements either the Iterator or the ListIterator interface. It enables you to cycle through a collection, removing or obtaining elements. The ListIterator extends Iterator to allow bidirectional traversal of a list, and the modification of elements.

Each of the collection classes provides an iterator( ) method that returns an iterator to the start of the collection. By using this iterator object, you can access each element in the collection. But it will be one element at a time.

Typically you need to follow the below mentioned steps in order to use an iterator to cycle through the contents if a collection –

a) Obtain an iterator to the start of collection by calling the collection's iterator ( ) method.

b) Set up a loop that makes a call to hasNext( ). Let the loop iterate as long as hasNext( ) returns true.

c) Obtain each element by calling next( ), within the loop.

You can also obtain an iterator by calling ListIterator, for collections that implement List.

The Methods declared by Iterator are as follows –

boolean hasNext( ) – if there are more elements it returns true, otherwise it returns false.

Object next( ) – It returns the next element and if there is no next element then it throws NoSuchElementException.

void remove( ) - This removes the current element. If an attempt is made to call remove() that is not preceded by a call to next( ) it throws IllegalStateException.

(TurtorialsPoint, 2017)

## Java Comparator

TreeSet and TreeMap, both store elements in sorted order, but it is the comparator that defines precisely what sorted order means. It defines two methods; equals( ) and compare( ).

equals( ) method – Suppose **obj** is the object to be tested for equality. The equals( ) method returns true if **obj** and invoking object are both Comparator objects and use the same ordering, false otherwise. The overriding equals( ) is unnecessary. Most of the simple comparators will not do so.

compare( ) method – Suppose two objects are two be compared (obj1 and obj2). If the objects are equal it will return zero. It returns a positive value in case obj1 is greater than obj2, negative value is returned otherwise. You can alter the way objects are ordered by using overriding compare( ). For example

– if you want to sort in reverse order, you can create a comparator that reverses the outcome of a comparison.

(TurtorialsPoint, 2017)

# Chapter 10
# Advanced SQL

Constraints

A constraint is a rule that is enforced on data columns in a table and they are used to limit what type of data can actually go into the table. This to ensure that the data in a database is reliable and accurate.

Constraints can be either column or table level. Column level will be applied to just one column, while table level is applied to the entire table. The following list is the most common constraints that SQL uses:

- NOT NULL Constraint – to ensure that a table cannot include a NULL value

- DEFAULT Constraint – to provide a default value on a column where there isn't one specified

- UNIQUE Constraint – to ensure that the values contained in a column are all different

- PRIMARY Key – to uniquely identify each of the rows and records in a table

- FOREIGN Key – to uniquely identify the rows and records in another table

- CHECK Constraint – to ensure that all of the values within a column satisfy specific conditions

- INDEX – to create data and retrieve it quickly from a database

A constraint can be specified when a table is first created, using the CREATE TABLE statement. You can also create the constraint after the table has been created by using the ALTER TABLE statement.

## Dropping Constraints:

You can drop any constraint that has been defined by using the ALTER TABLE command together with the option for DROP CONSTRAINT. For example, if you wanted to drop the primary key constraint from the EMPLOYEES table, you would use this command:

- ALTER TABLE EMPLOYEES DROP CONSTRAINT EMPLOYEES_PK;

Some of the implementations can give you a shortcut for dropping constraints. For example, if you wanted to drop the primary key constraint from an Oracle table, you would use this command:

- ALTER TABLE EMPLOYEES DROP PRIMARY KEY;

There are also implementations that allow you to disable a constraint, in case you don't want to permanently drop. Once disabled, the constraint can then be re-enabled later on.

## Integrity Constraints:

These are used to make sure that data in a relational database is accurate and consistent. The integrity of the data in a relational database is handled through the concept of referential integrity.

There are several different integrity constraint types that play a pat n RI – referential integrity. These include Foreign Key, Primary Key, Unique Key and all the others mentioned at the start of this chapter.

## Using Joins

The Joins in SQL is used when you want to combine the records from at least two tables together in a database. A JOIN is a way of combining the fields from tables using values that are common to each of them. Have a look at these two tables:

1. CUSTOMERS

```
+----+----------+-----+-----------+----------+
| ID | NAME     | AGE | ADDRESS   | SALARY   |
+----+----------+-----+-----------+----------+
| 1  | Ramesh   | 32  | Ahmedabad | 2000.00  |
| 2  | Khilan   | 25  | Delhi     | 1500.00  |
```

| 3 | kaushik | 23 | Kota | 2000.00 |

| 4 | Chaitali | 25 | Mumbai | 6500.00 |

| 5 | Hardik | 27 | Bhopal | 8500.00 |

| 6 | Komal | 22 | MP | 4500.00 |

| 7 | Muffy | 24 | Indore | 10000.00 |

+----+---------+-----+----------+---------+

2. ORDERS

+-----+-------------------+------------+--------+
|OID | DATE | CUSTOMER_ID | AMOUNT |
+-----+-------------------+------------+--------+

| 102 | 2009-10-08 00:00:00 | 3 | 3000 |

| 100 | 2009-10-08 00:00:00 | 3 | 1500 |

| 101 | 2009-11-20 00:00:00 | 2 | 1560 |

| 103 | 2008-05-20 00:00:00 | 4 | 2060 |

+-----+-------------------+------------+--------+

Use the SELECT statement to join the two tables together:

- SQL> SELECT ID, NAME, AGE, AMOUNT

- FROM CUSTOMERS, ORDERS

- WHERE CUSTOMERS.ID = ORDERS.CUSTOMER_ID;

Producing this result

```
+----+----------+-----+--------+
| ID | NAME     | AGE | AMOUNT |
+----+----------+-----+--------+
|  3 | kaushik  | 23  |  3000  |
|  3 | kaushik  | 23  |  1500  |
|  2 | Khilan   | 25  |  1560  |
|  4 | Chaitali | 25  |  2060  |
+----+----------+-----+--------+
```

Notice that the JOIN is performed within the WHERE clause. You can use a number of different operators to join a table, including:

- =

- <

- >

- <>

- <=

- \>=

- !=

- BETWEEN

- LIKE

- NOT

The most common one is the Equals symbol (=).

**SQL Join Types:**
There are several different JOIN types in SQL:

- INNER JOIN – will return a row or rows where a match is found in both tables.

- LEFT JOIN – will return all of the rows from the table on the left regardless of whether there are any matches in the right table

- RIGHT JOIN – will return all the rows from the right table, regardless of whether there are any matches in the left table

- FULL JOIN – will return all rows where there is a match found in any of the tables

- SELF JOIN – used to join one table to itself as if it were two tables, renaming at least one of them temporarily in the SQL statement

- CARTESIAN JOIN – will return the Cartesian product of the record sets from all of the joined tables

**UNIONS CLAUSE**

The UNION clause or operator is used when the results of at least two SELECT statements need to be combined without any duplicate rows being returned. When you use UNION, you must make sure that each SELECT has the eat same number of column selected, along with the same number of column expressions, data types and they must all be in the same order. They do not need to be the same length though.

The basic UNION syntax is:

- SELECT column1 [, column2 ]

- FROM table1 [, table2 ]

- [WHERE condition]

- UNION

- SELECT column1 [, column2 ]

- FROM table1 [, table2 ]

- [WHERE condition]

The given condition will be any expression that is based on your specific requirements.

Have a look at these two tables:

1. CUSTOMERS

```
+----+----------+-----+-----------+----------+
| ID | NAME     | AGE | ADDRESS   | SALARY   |
+----+----------+-----+-----------+----------+
| 1  | Ramesh   | 32  | Ahmedabad | 2000.00  |
| 2  | Khilan   | 25  | Delhi     | 1500.00  |
| 3  | kaushik  | 23  | Kota      | 2000.00  |
| 4  | Chaitali | 25  | Mumbai    | 6500.00  |
| 5  | Hardik   | 27  | Bhopal    | 8500.00  |
| 6  | Komal    | 22  | MP        | 4500.00  |
| 7  | Muffy    | 24  | Indore    | 10000.00 |
+----+----------+-----+-----------+----------+
```

2. ORDERS

```
+-----+---------------------+-------------+--------+
|OID  | DATE                | CUSTOMER_ID | AMOUNT |
+-----+---------------------+-------------+--------+
| 102 | 2009-10-08 00:00:00 |           3 |   3000 |
```

| 100 | 2009-10-08 00:00:00 |          3 |  1500 |

| 101 | 2009-11-20 00:00:00 |          2 |  1560 |

| 103 | 2008-05-20 00:00:00 |          4 |  2060 |

```
+-----+--------------------+------------+--------+
```

Join the tables together in your SELECT statement.

- SQL> SELECT ID, NAME, AMOUNT, DATE

- FROM CUSTOMERS

- LEFT JOIN ORDERS

- ON CUSTOMERS.ID = ORDERS.CUSTOMER_ID

- UNION

- SELECT ID, NAME, AMOUNT, DATE

- FROM CUSTOMERS

- RIGHT JOIN ORDERS

- ON CUSTOMERS.ID = ORDERS.CUSTOMER_ID;

Producing the following result

```
+------+----------+--------+--------------------+
```

| ID  | NAME    | AMOUNT | DATE               |

```
+------+----------+--------+--------------------+
|  1 | Ramesh  |  NULL | NULL               |
|  2 | Khilan  |  1560 | 2009-11-20 00:00:00 |
|  3 | kaushik |  3000 | 2009-10-08 00:00:00 |
|  3 | kaushik |  1500 | 2009-10-08 00:00:00 |
|  4 | Chaitali |  2060 | 2008-05-20 00:00:00 |
|  5 | Hardik  |  NULL | NULL               |
|  6 | Komal   |  NULL | NULL               |
|  7 | Muffy   |  NULL | NULL               |
+------+----------+--------+--------------------+
```

**The UNION ALL Clause:**

This operator or clause is used when you want to combine the results from two SELECT statements, including any duplicate rows. The rules that we use for UNION apply to UNION ALL.

The basic syntax from the UNION ALL clause i:

- SELECT column1 [, column2 ]

- FROM table1 [, table2 ]

- [WHERE condition]

- UNION ALL

- SELECT column1 [, column2 ]

- FROM table1 [, table2 ]

- [WHERE condition]

The given condition will be any expression based on your specific requirements.

Take a look at these two tables:

1. CUSTOMERS

```
+----+----------+-----+-----------+----------+
| ID | NAME     | AGE | ADDRESS   | SALARY   |
+----+----------+-----+-----------+----------+
| 1  | Ramesh   | 32  | Ahmedabad | 2000.00  |
| 2  | Khilan   | 25  | Delhi     | 1500.00  |
| 3  | kaushik  | 23  | Kota      | 2000.00  |
| 4  | Chaitali | 25  | Mumbai    | 6500.00  |
| 5  | Hardik   | 27  | Bhopal    | 8500.00  |
| 6  | Komal    | 22  | MP        | 4500.00  |
| 7  | Muffy    | 24  | Indore    | 10000.00 |
+----+----------+-----+-----------+----------+
```

2. ORDERS

```
+-----+-------------------+------------+--------+
|OID  | DATE              | CUSTOMER_ID | AMOUNT |
+-----+-------------------+------------+--------+
| 102 | 2009-10-08 00:00:00 |        3 |  3000 |
| 100 | 2009-10-08 00:00:00 |        3 |  1500 |
| 101 | 2009-11-20 00:00:00 |        2 |  1560 |
| 103 | 2008-05-20 00:00:00 |        4 |  2060 |
+-----+-------------------+------------+--------+
```

Join the tables together in your SELECT statement.

- SQL> SELECT  ID, NAME, AMOUNT, DATE

- FROM CUSTOMERS

- LEFT JOIN ORDERS

- ON CUSTOMERS.ID = ORDERS.CUSTOMER_ID

- UNION ALL

- SELECT  ID, NAME, AMOUNT, DATE

- FROM CUSTOMERS

- RIGHT JOIN ORDERS

- ON CUSTOMERS.ID = ORDERS.CUSTOMER_ID;

Producing this result

```
+------+----------+--------+---------------------+
| ID   | NAME     | AMOUNT | DATE                |
+------+----------+--------+---------------------+
|  1   | Ramesh   |  NULL  | NULL                |
|  2   | Khilan   |  1560  | 2009-11-20 00:00:00 |
|  3   | kaushik  |  3000  | 2009-10-08 00:00:00 |
|  3   | kaushik  |  1500  | 2009-10-08 00:00:00 |
|  4   | Chaitali |  2060  | 2008-05-20 00:00:00 |
|  5   | Hardik   |  NULL  | NULL                |
|  6   | Komal    |  NULL  | NULL                |
|  7   | Muffy    |  NULL  | NULL                |
|  3   | kaushik  |  3000  | 2009-10-08 00:00:00 |
|  3   | kaushik  |  1500  | 2009-10-08 00:00:00 |
|  2   | Khilan   |  1560  | 2009-11-20 00:00:00 |
|  4   | Chaitali |  2060  | 2008-05-20 00:00:00 |
+------+----------+--------+---------------------+
```

There are two more operators that are similar to UNION:

- SQL INTERSECT Clause is used to combine two SELECT statements, but will return the rows from just the first one if they are identical to any in the second statement.

- SQL EXCEPT Clause – this combine two SELECT statements and will return rows from the first statement if they are not returned by the second

**NULL Values**

NULL is the SQL term used to represent a missing value. NULL values appear in a table field that looks blank, in essence, being a field that has no value. Do not mistake a NULL value with a zero value or a field that has spaces in it.

The basic syntax for NULL when you are creating a table is:

- SQL> CREATE TABLE CUSTOMERS(

- ID  INT        NOT NULL,

- NAME VARCHAR (20)    NOT NULL,

- AGE  INT        NOT NULL,

- ADDRESS  CHAR (25) ,

- SALARY   DECIMAL (18, 2),

- PRIMARY KEY (ID)

- );

NOT NULL is used to signify that a specific column must always except explicit values of a specified data type. In the columns where NOT NUL is not used, they could be interpreted as being NULL. A field that has a NULL value is one that has been left blank when the record was being created.

The NULL value can cause a few problems when it comes to selecting data because, when you compare one unknown value to another value, the result will always come up as unknown and will not be included in the results.

If you want to check for a NULL value, you must always use the IS NULL or IS NOT NULL operators.

Look at the following table

CUSTOMERS

```
+----+----------+-----+-----------+----------+
| ID | NAME     | AGE | ADDRESS   | SALARY   |
+----+----------+-----+-----------+----------+
|  1 | Ramesh   |  32 | Ahmedabad |  2000.00 |
|  2 | Khilan   |  25 | Delhi     |  1500.00 |
|  3 | kaushik  |  23 | Kota      |  2000.00 |
```

| 4 | Chaitali | 25 | Mumbai  | 6500.00 |

| 5 | Hardik  | 27 | Bhopal  | 8500.00 |

| 6 | Komal   | 22 | MP      |         |

| 7 | Muffy   | 24 | Indore  |         |

+----+----------+-----+-----------+----------+

The following is an example of using the NOT NULL operator

- SQL> SELECT  ID, NAME, AGE, ADDRESS, SALARY

- FROM CUSTOMERS

- WHERE SALARY IS NOT NULL;

Producing this result

+----+----------+-----+-----------+----------+

| ID | NAME    | AGE | ADDRESS  | SALARY  |

+----+----------+-----+-----------+----------+

| 1 | Ramesh  | 32 | Ahmedabad | 2000.00 |

| 2 | Khilan  | 25 | Delhi    | 1500.00 |

| 3 | kaushik | 23 | Kota     | 2000.00 |

| 4 | Chaitali | 25 | Mumbai   | 6500.00 |

| 5 | Hardik  | 27 | Bhopal   | 8500.00 |

```
+----+----------+-----+-----------+----------+
```

This is an example of the IS NULL operator

- SQL> SELECT ID, NAME, AGE, ADDRESS, SALARY

- FROM CUSTOMERS

- WHERE SALARY IS NULL;

Producing this result

```
+----+----------+-----+-----------+----------+
| ID | NAME     | AGE | ADDRESS   | SALARY   |
+----+----------+-----+-----------+----------+
| 6  | Komal    | 22  | MP        |          |
| 7  | Muffy    | 24  | Indore    |          |
+----+----------+-----+-----------+----------+
```

**Alias Syntax**

It is possible to temporarily rename a column or a table by using ALIAS. Using table aliases means that you are renaming a table in a specific SQL statement. It is a temporary change only and the database will not reflect the change, showing only the original name. Column aliases are used when you want to rename the columns in a table for a specific SQL query.

The basic syntax of table alias is:

- SELECT column1, column2....

- FROM table_name AS alias_name

- WHERE [condition];

The basic syntax of column alias is

- SELECT column_name AS alias_name

- FROM table_name

- WHERE [condition];

Take a look at these two tables

1. CUSTOMERS

```
+----+----------+-----+-----------+----------+
| ID | NAME     | AGE | ADDRESS   | SALARY   |
+----+----------+-----+-----------+----------+
| 1  | Ramesh   | 32  | Ahmedabad | 2000.00  |
| 2  | Khilan   | 25  | Delhi     | 1500.00  |
| 3  | kaushik  | 23  | Kota      | 2000.00  |
| 4  | Chaitali | 25  | Mumbai    | 6500.00  |
| 5  | Hardik   | 27  | Bhopal    | 8500.00  |
| 6  | Komal    | 22  | MP        | 4500.00  |
```

| 7 | Muffy  | 24 | Indore  | 10000.00 |

+----+----------+-----+-----------+----------+

2. ORDERS

+-----+-------------------+-------------+--------+

|OID | DATE           | CUSTOMER_ID | AMOUNT |

+-----+-------------------+-------------+--------+

| 102 | 2009-10-08 00:00:00 |     3 |  3000 |

| 100 | 2009-10-08 00:00:00 |     3 |  1500 |

| 101 | 2009-11-20 00:00:00 |     2 |  1560 |

| 103 | 2008-05-20 00:00:00 |     4 |  2060 |

+-----+-------------------+-------------+--------+

This is how to use the table alias

- SQL> SELECT C.ID, C.NAME, C.AGE, O.AMOUNT

- FROM CUSTOMERS AS C, ORDERS AS O

- WHERE  C.ID = O.CUSTOMER_ID;

Producing this result

+----+----------+-----+--------+

| ID | NAME    | AGE | AMOUNT |

```
+----+----------+-----+--------+

| 3 | kaushik  | 23 |  3000 |

| 3 | kaushik  | 23 |  1500 |

| 2 | Khilan   | 25 |  1560 |

| 4 | Chaitali | 25 |  2060 |

+----+----------+-----+--------+
```

This is how to use column alias

- SQL> SELECT   ID AS CUSTOMER_ID, NAME AS CUSTOMER_NAME

- FROM CUSTOMERS

- WHERE SALARY IS NOT NULL;

Producing this result

```
+-------------+---------------+

| CUSTOMER_ID | CUSTOMER_NAME |

+-------------+---------------+

|           1 | Ramesh        |

|           2 | Khilan        |

|           3 | kaushik       |
```

```
|     4 | Chaitali   |

|     5 | Hardik     |

|     6 | Komal      |

|     7 | Muffy      |

+-------------+---------------+
```

## Indexes

An index is a lookup table that is used by the database search engine to speed up the retrieval of data. An index points to specific data in a table and is similar to the index you find in a book.

For example, if you wanted to reference all the page in a book that talked about a specific topic, you would look at the index. This lists the book topic in alphabetical order, referring a reader to specific page numbers.

An index also helps to speed up WHERE clauses and SELECT queries but it does slow down the input of data with the INSERT and UPDATE statements. You can create or drop an index with absolutely no effect on a table.

To create an index, you use the CREATE INDEX statement. This lets you give the index a name, specify the table and the columns to be indexed and to indicate the order of the index, either descending or ascending order.

Similar to the UNIQUE constraint, indexes may also be unique in that it may prevent duplicate entries from being in the columns where there is an index.

**The CREATE INDEX Command:**

The basic syntax of CREATE INDEX is

- CREATE INDEX index_name ON table_name;

**Single-Column Indexes:**

Single column indexes are created based on a single column. The basic syntax is:

- CREATE INDEX index_name

- ON table_name (column_name);

**Unique Indexes:**

A unique index is used for performance and for data integrity. It will not let any duplicate values be put into the table. The basic syntax is

- CREATE UNIQUE INDEX index_name

- on table_name (column_name);

**Composite Indexes:**

Composite indexes are indexes on at least two columns in a table. The basic syntax is

- CREATE INDEX index_name

- on table_name (column1, column2);

No matter whether you are creating a composite on a single column index, consider carefully the columns that you might use on a frequent bass in the WHERE clause when you are setting the filter conditions. If there is only a single column to be used, the choice should be a single column index. Where two or more are used, choose the composite index.

## Implicit Indexes:

An Implicit index is one that is created automatically by the server when objects are created. An index is created automatically for unique and primary key constraints.

## The DROP INDEX Command:

You can drop an index by using the DROP command in SQL. Do take care when you are doing this as it may have an effect on performance. The basic syntax is

- DROP INDEX index_name;

## When to Avoid Indexes

On the whole, indexes should enhance the performance of a database but, like anything, there are times that you should avoid using them. These guidelines give you an idea of whether or not you should consider using an index:

- You should not use an index on a small table

- You should not use indexes on table that have these

operations – Insert, Large Batch update or Frequent

- You should not use an index on a column that contains a large number of NULL values

- You should not use an index on a column that is manipulated frequently

**ALTER TABLE Command**

We use the ALTER TABLE command on an existing table to add, modify or delete columns. You can also use it to add or drop constraints to an existing table. The basic syntax to add a column to an existing table is

- ALTER TABLE table_name ADD column_name datatype;

The syntax for ALTER TABLE to DROP COLUMN in an existing table is

- ALTER TABLE table_name DROP COLUMN column_name;

The syntax for changing the DATA TYPE of a column is

- ALTER TABLE table_name MODIFY COLUMN column_name datatype;

The syntax for add a NOT NULL constraint is

- ALTER TABLE table_name MODIFY column_name datatype NOT NULL;

The syntax for ADD UNIQUE CONSTRAINT is

- ALTER TABLE table_name

- ADD CONSTRAINT MyUniqueConstraint UNIQUE(column1, column2...);

The syntax for ADD CHEK CONSTRAINT is

- ALTER TABLE table_name

- ADD CONSTRAINT MyUniqueConstraint CHECK (CONDITION);

The syntax for ADD PRMARY KEY is

- ALTER TABLE table_name

- ADD CONSTRAINT MyPrimaryKey PRIMARY KEY (column1, column2...);

The syntax of DROP CONSTRAINT is

- ALTER TABLE table_name

- DROP CONSTRAINT MyUniqueConstraint;

If you use MySQL you would use this code

- ALTER TABLE table_name

- DROP INDEX MyUniqueConstraint;

The syntax for DROP PRIMARY KEY is

- ALTER TABLE table_name

- DROP CONSTRAINT MyPrimaryKey;

If you use MySQL, the code is

- ALTER TABLE table_name

- DROP PRIMARY KEY;

Have a look at these tables

CUSTOMERS

```
+----+----------+-----+----------+----------+
| ID | NAME     | AGE | ADDRESS  | SALARY   |
+----+----------+-----+----------+----------+
| 1  | Ramesh   | 32  | Ahmedabad| 2000.00  |
| 2  | Khilan   | 25  | Delhi    | 1500.00  |
| 3  | kaushik  | 23  | Kota     | 2000.00  |
| 4  | Chaitali | 25  | Mumbai   | 6500.00  |
| 5  | Hardik   | 27  | Bhopal   | 8500.00  |
| 6  | Komal    | 22  | MP       | 4500.00  |
| 7  | Muffy    | 24  | Indore   | 10000.00 |
+----+----------+-----+----------+----------+
```

This is how you would ADD in a new column to the table

- ALTER TABLE CUSTOMERS ADD SEX char(1);

The CUSTOMERS table has now been changed and this would be the output from the SELECT statement

```
+----+---------+-----+-----------+----------+------+
| ID | NAME    | AGE | ADDRESS   | SALARY   | SEX  |
+----+---------+-----+-----------+----------+------+
|  1 | Ramesh  |  32 | Ahmedabad |  2000.00 | NULL |
|  2 | Ramesh  |  25 | Delhi     |  1500.00 | NULL |
|  3 | kaushik |  23 | Kota      |  2000.00 | NULL |
|  4 | kaushik |  25 | Mumbai    |  6500.00 | NULL |
|  5 | Hardik  |  27 | Bhopal    |  8500.00 | NULL |
|  6 | Komal   |  22 | MP        |  4500.00 | NULL |
|  7 | Muffy   |  24 | Indore    | 10000.00 | NULL |
+----+---------+-----+-----------+----------+------+
```

This is how to DROP a column from the table, in this case "sex"

- ALTER TABLE CUSTOMERS DROP SEX;

The CUSTOEMRS table has now been changed and this is the

output from the SELECT statement

```
+----+---------+-----+-----------+----------+
| ID | NAME    | AGE | ADDRESS   | SALARY   |
+----+---------+-----+-----------+----------+
| 1  | Ramesh  | 32  | Ahmedabad | 2000.00  |
| 2  | Ramesh  | 25  | Delhi     | 1500.00  |
| 3  | kaushik | 23  | Kota      | 2000.00  |
| 4  | kaushik | 25  | Mumbai    | 6500.00  |
| 5  | Hardik  | 27  | Bhopal    | 8500.00  |
| 6  | Komal   | 22  | MP        | 4500.00  |
| 7  | Muffy   | 24  | Indore    | 10000.00 |
+----+---------+-----+-----------+----------+
```

# Chapter 11
# Advanced C++

C++ Files and Streams

The iostream standard C++ library provides the methods cin and cout for reading standard inputs and writing standard outputs. However, you can use fstream, another standard library, to read and write from files. Fstream defines three new types of data:

| Data Type | Description |
|-----------|-------------|
| ofstream | This represents an output file stream, used to create a file and write information to a file |
| ifstream | This represent an input file, used to read from files |
| fstream | This represents the file stream in general and use the capabilities from ofstream and ifstream. This mean it can create a file, write information to a file and read from a file. |

If you want to process files n C++, you have to use the header files <iostream> and <fstream> in your source file.

**Opening a File:**

A file has to be opened up before you can read from or write to it. You can use either ofstream of fstream to open up a file for writing to while, for reading only you would use ifstream.

The standard syntax for the open() function, a member of the objects fstream, ifstream and ofstream, is

- void open(const char *filename, ios::openmcode mcode);

The first argument in this syntax specifies both the name and the location of file that is to be opened. The second argument of the open() function is defining the mcode that should be used to open the file in.

| Mcode Flag | Description |
| --- | --- |
| ios::app | This is Append Mcode. Any output to the file will be appended to the end of the file. |
| ios::ate | Allows you to open a file for output and then move the control for read/write to the end |
| ios::in | Allows you to open a file for reading purposes |
| ios::out | Allows you to open a file for writing purposes |
| ios::trunc | If the file specified exits already, the contents of it will be truncated before the file is opened |

It is possible to combine at least two of these values together by using OR. For example, if you wanted to open up a file in Write mcode and then wanted to Truncate it, should it already exist, you would use this syntax:

- ofstream outfile;

- outfile.open("file.dat", ios::out | ios::trunc );

Similarly, you could also open up a file for both reading and writing like this:

- fstream afile;

- afile.open("file.dat", ios::out | ios::in );

## Closing a File

When a program in C++ terminates, it will automatically flush out all stream, release any memory that has been allocated and close down any files that are open. But, you should get into the habit of closing down open files before you terminate the program. To do this, use the following standard syntax for the close() function, a member of the objects fstream, ifstream and ofstream:

- void close();

## Writing to a File:

When you are programming in C++, you will write information to files from the program by using (<<), the stream insertion operator in the same way that you would use the operator to send output to your screen The only difference here is that you would use the objects ofstream or fstream instead of using cout.

## Reading from a File:

Information from a file can be read to a program by using the (>>) stream extraction operator in the same way that you sue the operator to input information using a keyboard. The difference is that you use the objects ifstream or fstream instead of cin.

## Read & Write Example:

The following program is a C++ program that will open up a file in both read and write mcode. After the Write information has been input to a file called afile.dat, by the user, the program will then read the information and output it to the screen:

- #include <fstream>

- #include <iostream>

- using namespace std;

- int main ()

- {

- char data[100];

- // open a file in write mcode.

- ofstream outfile;

- outfile.open("afile.dat");

- cout << "Writing to the file" << endl;

- cout << "Enter your name: ";

- cin.getline(data, 100);

- // write inputted data into the file.

- outfile << data << endl;

- cout << "Enter your age: ";

- cin >> data;

- cin.ignore();

- // again write inputted data into the file.

- outfile << data << endl;

- // close the opened file.

- outfile.close();

- // open a file in read mcode.

- ifstream infile;

- infile.open("afile.dat");

- cout << "Reading from the file" << endl;

- infile >> data;

- // write the data at the screen.

- cout << data << endl;

- // again read the data from the file and display it.

- infile >> data;

- cout << data << endl;

- // close the opened file.

- infile.close();

- return 0;

- }

When you compile the above code and then execute it, you will see the following input and output:

- $./a.out

- Writing to the file

- Enter your name: Zara

- Enter your age: 9

- Reading from the file

- Zara

- 9

These examples use extra functions from the object cin, like the getline() function that is used to read the line outside, and the ignore() function which ignores any extra characters that have been left by the last read statement.

## File Position Pointers

Ifstream and ofstream will both provide member functions for help in positioning the file-position pointer. Those member functions are seekp (seek put) for ofstream and seekg (seek get) for ifstream. Usually, the argument for both of these would be a very long integer. Another argument can also be specified to sow the seek position. The direction of seek can be ios::beg, which is the default, for positioning in relation to the start of a stream; ios::cur for positioning that is in relation to the current position and ios::end for positioning in relation to the end of the stream.

A file-position pointer is always an integer value that will specify the file location as a byte number, indicating how far from the start position the file is. Some examples of using the get file position pointer are:

- // position to the nth byte of fileObject (assumes ios::beg)

- fileObject.seekg( n );

- // position n bytes forward in fileObject

- fileObject.seekg( n, ios::cur );

- // position n bytes back from end of fileObject

- fileObject.seekg( n, ios::end );

- // position at end of fileObject

- fileObject.seekg( 0, ios::end );

# C++ Exception Handling

An exception is something that may arise when a program is being executed. Exceptions are responses to something that arises when the program is running. They are usually exceptional circumstances, for example, an attempt at division by zero.

They provide a way of transferring control from one bit of a program to another bit and it is built in three different keywords – try, throw and catch.

- **throw** – a program will throw up an exception whenever there is a problem, done with the use of the throw keyword.

- **catch** – a program will catch an exception with the use of an exception handler at the point in a program where you want the problem handled. The catch keyword is used to indicate this.

- **try** – try blocks are used to identify code blocks for which a specific exception is going to be activated. It will always be followed by at least one catch block.

Assuming that a particular bloc is going to raise an exception, a method will catch that exception by using both the catch and try keywords. A try/catch block will be placed around the particular code that could raise an exception and any code within the block is known as "protected" code. The syntax for a try/catch block is similar to:

- try

- {

- // protected code

- }catch( ExceptionName e1 )

- {

- // catch block

- }catch( ExceptionName e2 )

- {

- // catch block

- }catch( ExceptionName eN )

- {

- // catch block

- }

You may list several catch statements to try and catch all different exception types in the event that your try block raises several exceptions in different situations.

**Throwing Exceptions:**

An exception may be thrown anywhere in a code block that uses throw statements. The throw statement operand will determine an exception type and may be any expression. The result type of the expression will determine the exception type that is thrown.

The following example shows a thrown exception when a condition whereby a division by zero is asked for occurs:

- double division(int a, int b)

- {

- if( b == 0 )

- {

- throw "Division by zero condition!";

- }

- return (a/b);

- }

## Catching Exceptions:

When you follow a try block with a catch block, it will capture any and all exceptions. You are able to specify the type of exception that you want to catch, determined by the declaration from the exception that is shown in the parentheses after the catch keyword.

- try

- {

- // protected code

- }catch( ExceptionName e )

- {

- // code to handle ExceptionName exception

- }

The code above will catch any exception of the type ExceptionName. If you wanted to specify that a catch block must handle all exception types that are thrown in a try block, you must use an ellipsis (...) in between the parentheses that enclose the exception declaration:

- try

- {

- // protected code

- }catch(...)

- {

- // code to handle any exception

- }

The next example shows a thrown exception of the divide by zero type, which is then caught in a catch block:

```cpp
#include <iostream>

using namespace std;

double division(int a, int b)

{

if( b == 0 )

{

throw "Division by zero condition!";

}

return (a/b);

}

int main ()

{

int x = 50;

int y = 0;

double z = 0;

try {

z = division(x, y);
```

- cout << z << endl;

- }catch (const char* msg) {

- cerr << msg << endl;

- }

- return 0;

- }

In this example we have raised an exception of the const char* type meaning that we must use const char* in the catch block to catch the exception If we were to compile that example above and run it, we would get this result:

- Division by zero condition!

**C++ Standard Exceptions:**
C++ gives us a list of the standard exceptions that are defined in <exception> that can be used in the programs we write. The exceptions are arranged in a hierarchy of parent-child class and the following table shows a description of the exceptions in the hierarchy:

| Exception | Description |
| --- | --- |
| **std::exception** | This is an exception and is the parent class of all standard exceptions in C++ |
| std::bad_alloc | This exception can be thrown by the keyword new |
| std::bad_cast | This exception can be thrown by dynamic_cast |
| std::bad_exception | This exception is useful in handling unexpected exceptions |
| std::bad_typeid | This exception can be thrown by typeid |
| **std::logic_error** | This exception can, in theory, be detected just by reading a piece of code |
| std::domain_error | This exception is thrown when a domain that is mathematically invalid is used. |
| std::invalid_argument | This exception is thrown up because of invalid arguments |
| std::length_error | This exception is thrown up when an std::string that is too large is created |

| std::out_of_range | This exception may be thrown up by the at() method from, for example, an std::bitset, std::vector, <>:: and the operators [] () |
|---|---|
| **std::runtime_error** | This is an exception that, in theory, cannot be detected jut by reading the code |
| std::overflow_error | This exception is thrown when a mathematical overflow happens |
| std::range_error | This exception will occur when you attempt to store values that are out of range |
| std::underflow_error | This exception will be thrown when an instance of mathematical underflow happens |

## Define New Exceptions:

You may define your own exceptions by inheriting the exception class functionality and overriding it. The following example shows you how to use the std::exception class when you want to implement your exception in a standard manner:

- #include <iostream>

- #include <exception>

- using namespace std;

```cpp
struct MyException : public exception

{

const char * what () const throw ()

{

return "C++ Exception";

}

};

int main()

{

try

{

throw MyException();

}

catch(MyException& e)

{

std::cout << "MyException caught" << std::endl;

std::cout << e.what() << std::endl;
```

- }

- catch(std::exception& e)

- {

- //Other errors

- }

- }

Compiling and then executing this code will produce this result:

- MyException caught

- C++ Exception

In this example, what() is a public method that has been provided by the exception class and overridden by every child exception class, thus returning what caused an exception.

**Dynamic Memory**

If you want to become a good C++ programmer, you must have a decent and sound understanding of how dynamic memory work. The memory in any C++ program is divided up into 2 parts:

- **The stack** – all of the variables that are declared inside a function will use memory from the stack

- **The heap** – the unused memory of any C++ program, used

when allocating memory dynamically when your program is run

Much of the time, you will not know up front how much memory is going to be needed for storing information in a defined variable. The size of the memory will be determined when it comes time to run the program.

Memory can be allocated in the heap at run-time for any variable of a specified type, with the use of a special C++ operator. This operator will return the address of the space to be allocated and is called the new operator.

If you no longer need to use dynamically allocated memory, using the delete operator will deallocate any memory that was allocated previously by the new operator.

**The new and delete operators:**
The following shows the standard syntax for using the new operator to dynamically allocate memory for any specified data type:

* new data-type;

In this syntax, the data type can be any data type that is built in, including arrays or any data type that is user-defined, including classes or structures. Let's look at the built-in data types. We could define a pointer that types double and then we could request that the memory is allocated at the time of execution We use the new operator to do this, using these statements:

- double* pvalue = NULL; // Pointer initialized with null

- pvalue = new double;  // Request memory for the variable

It may not be possible to allocate the memory successfully if the free storage has already been used. So, you should get into the habit of checking that the new operator is actually returning a NULL pointer and then take this action:

- double* pvalue = NULL;

- if( !(pvalue = new double ))

- {

- cout << "Error: out of memory." <<endl;

- exit(1);

- }

Some of you may remember the malloc() function used in C. This is still in C++ but it isn't recommended for use. The biggest advantage of using new instead of malloc() is that it won't just allocate memory; instead it will also construct objects and this is the main purpose of the C++ language.

When you determine that a variable, that has already been dynamically allocated, is no longer required, you may use the delete operator to free up that memory:

- delete pvalue;      // Release memory pointed to by pvalue

Let's put these concepts to the test. The following example show how the new and delete operator work:

- #include <iostream>

- using namespace std;

- int main ()

- {

- double* pvalue = NULL; // Pointer initialized with null

- pvalue = new double;  // Request memory for the variable

- *pvalue = 29494.99;    // Store value at allocated address

- cout << "Value of pvalue : " << *pvalue << endl;

- delete pvalue;      // free up the memory.

- return 0;

- }

If you compile this code and execute it, you will get the following result:

- Value of pvalue : 29495

## Dynamic Memory Allocation for Arrays:

If you wanted to allocate memory for a character array, i.e. a string of 20 character, you would use the same syntax from the above example to dynamically allocate the memory:

- char* pvalue = NULL;  // Pointer initialized with null

- pvalue = new char[20]; // Request memory for the variable

If you were to remove the array you created, your statement would look like:

- delete [] pvalue;      // Delete array pointed to by pvalue

The following shows the syntax for the new operator in a multi-dimensional array:

- int ROW = 2;

- int COL = 3;

- double **pvalue = new double* [ROW]; // Allocate memory for rows

- // Now allocate memory for columns

- for(int i = 0; i < COL; i++) {

- pvalue[i] = new double[COL];

- }

And the syntax you would use for releasing the memory for a multi-dimensional array is:

- for(int i = 0; i < COL; i++) {

- delete[] pvalue[i];

- }

- delete [] pvalue;

**Dynamic Memory Allocation for Objects:**

An object is no different to a simple data type. For example, look at the following code where we use an array of objects as a way of clarifying the concept:

- #include <iostream>

- using namespace std;

- class Box

- {

- public:

- Box() {

- cout << "Constructor called!" <<endl;

- }

- ~Box() {

- cout << "Destructor called!" <<endl;

- }

- };

- int main( )

- {

- Box* myBoxArray = new Box[4];

- delete [] myBoxArray; // Delete array

- return 0;

- }

Let's say that you were going to allocate an array containing four Box objects. The Simple constructor would, as a result, be called four times. In a similar manner, while you were deleting the objects, the destructor would also be called four times.

If you were to compile the above example and then run it, you would get this result:

- Constructor called!

- Constructor called!

- Constructor called!

- Constructor called!

- Destructor called!

- Destructor called!

- Destructor called!

- Destructor called!

**Namespaces in C++**

Let's say that we have two people who both have the same name, Zara, and they are both in the same class. Whenever you need to differentiate between them, you would need to use some additional information, as well as the name. For example, you could use the area they are living in, their mother's name, father's name, age, etc.

The same thing can happen in a C++ application. For example, you could be writing a piece of code that includes a function named xyz(). There may be another library that also has that same function in it. The compiler would not know which xyz() your code is referring to.

In this case, we would use a namespace. These are used also to provide extra information to differentiate between identical or similar functions, variables, classes, etc., that have the same names in different libraries. By using namespace, you are able to define the context of a name, or, in other words, define the scope.

**Defining a Namespace:**

Namespace definitions start with the namespace keyword and are followed by the name:

- namespace namespace_name {

- // code declarations

- }

In order to call the namespace version of a variable or a function, the namespace name must be prepended:

- name::code; // code could be variable or function.

The following examples show the namespace scopes of certain entities, including functions and variables:

- #include <iostream>

- using namespace std;

- // first name space

- namespace first_space{

- void func(){

- cout << "Inside first_space" << endl;

- }

- }

- // second name space

- namespace second_space{

- void func(){

- cout << "Inside second_space" << endl;

- }

- }

- int main ()

- {

- // Calls function from first name space.

- first_space::func();

- // Calls function from second name space.

- second_space::func();

- return 0;

- }

If you compile this code and then execute it, you get this result:

- Inside first_space

- Inside second_space

**The using directive:**

If you use the using namespace directive, you do not need to prepend your namespaces. The directive tells your compiler that the code is using names that are inside a specified namespace, which is implied in the code:

- #include <iostream>

- using namespace std;

- // first name space

- namespace first_space{

- void func(){

- cout << "Inside first_space" << endl;

- }

- }

- // second name space

- namespace second_space{

- void func(){

- cout << "Inside second_space" << endl;

- }

- }

- using namespace first_space;

- int main ()

- {

- // This calls function from first name space.

- func();

- return 0;

- }

Compiling and executing this code gives this result:

- Inside first_space

This directive can also be used as a way of referencing a specific item in a namespace. For example, if you only wanted to use the cout part of an std namespace, you would refer to it as

- using std::cout;

Any subsequent code would refer to cout without needing to prepend the namespace but, if there are other terms in the std namespace they must still be explicit:

- #include <iostream>

- using std::cout;

- int main ()

- {

- cout << "std::endl is used with std!" << std::endl;

- return 0;

- }

Compiling and executing this code will give you this result:

- std::endl is used with std!

A name that is introduced in a using directive will obey al of the normal scope rules. The name will be visible from the using directive through to the end of the scope the directive is in. Entities that have the same name but that are defined in an outer cope will be hidden.

**Discontiguous Namespaces:**
Namespaces can be defined in a number of parts and is, as a result, made up of the sum of all of the parts. Each part may be spread over a number of files. So, if one of the parts needs a name that is defined inside another file, the name still has to be declared. The following example of a namespace definitions will either add elements to an existing namespace or will define a new one:

- namespace namespace_name {

- // code declarations

- }

**Nested Namespaces:**

You can nest a namespace, which means that you can define one inside another, as such:

- namespace namespace_name1 {

- // code declarations

- namespace namespace_name2 {

- // code declarations

- }

- }

Accessing the members of a nested namespace is done by using resolution operators, like this:

- // to access members of namespace_name2

- using namespace namespace_name1::namespace_name2;

- // to access members of namespace:name1

- using namespace namespace_name1;

In the example statement, if you use namespace_name1, it makes the elements of namespace_name2 available inside the scope:

```cpp
#include <iostream>

using namespace std;

// first name space

namespace first_space{

void func(){

cout << "Inside first_space" << endl;

}

// second name space

namespace second_space{

void func(){

cout << "Inside second_space" << endl;

}

}

}

using namespace first_space::second_space;

int main ()

{
```

- // This calls function from second name space.

- func();

- return 0;

- }

Compiling this example and executing it will give us this result

- Inside second_space

## C++ Templates

A template is a blueprint or formula for creating a generic class or function. The library containers like algorithms and iterators are examples of generic programming. In other words, templates are the foundation of generic programming, which involves writing a code in such a way that is independent of any particular type. The templates can be used to define functions as well as classes.

## Standard Library in C++

The standard library in C++ can be categorized into two parts –

a) Object-Oriented Class library – It is a collection of associated functions and classes.

b) Standard Function Library – It consists of stand-alone, general-purpose functions that are not part of any class. Function library is inherited from C language.

The standard C++ library incorporates all the standard C libraries as well. However, there are small additions and changes to support type safety.

The Object-Oriented Class library defines a widespread set of classes that provide support for a number of common activities, including strings, I/O, and numeric processing. This library includes the following –

a) The string class

b) Standard C++ I/O classes

c) Numeric classes

d) aaaaSTL container classes

e) STL algorithms

f) STL Function Objects

g) STL allocators

h) Localization library

i) Exception handling library

j) Miscellaneous support library

The standard function library has been divided into the following categories –

a) String and Character handling

b) I/O

c) Mathematical

d) Dynamic Allocation

e) Time, Date and Allocation

f) Miscellaneous

g) Wide character Functions

Sample coding courtesy of TutorialsPoint.com

# Chapter 12
# Useful Tips for Programmers

Becoming a programmer is a cumulative process that helps in building up your skills gradually; programming can be fun and rewarding. Here, we are listing some useful tips which would help you to make a transition from beginner to an experienced developer.

1. Learn new programming language – Irrespective of how many programming languages you already know, but learning a new language will always help you to become a better developer. Learning a new language consists of three realms of knowledge; the syntax, built-in operators and libraries and method of using them. Learning syntax, operators and libraries are just a matter of slowly accumulating knowledge but the method of using them can only be learned over months of working with a language. We advise that you can do a project that is well suited for that language and its style. (james, 2009)

2. Learn advanced search techniques, strategies and tactics – Modern languages and development frameworks are too large for most people to remember everything. As a result, the ability to get work done is often dependent on the ability

to perform research. The techniques that you need to learn as a developer are the advanced search systems of your favorite search engine; learn things such as Boolean operators, how to filter results and what role word order plays and more. The tactics which you need to learn such as knowing how to approach any particular search and knowing what you should actually look for. As far as strategies are concerned, you need to learn things such as what search engines to use, which sites to visit before going to general purpose search engine.

3. Be patient and keep practicing – We all know for that fact that it takes a lot of time and energy to become an expert. Therefore the key is to keep practicing and keep patience to reap the benefits of your hard work.

4. Don't just read the sample code, play with it – Reading sample codes is not enough to understand how it works. In order to develop a true understanding you actually need to run the code and play with it. This will facilitate the learning process much more than just by reading it.

5. Take breaks when debugging – When debugging, we sit for hours trying to solve the issue but there is no guarantee that the problem will get fixed. The best step is to step away from the bug for a couple of hours and return with a fresh perspective. This much-needed break will surely improve your productivity.

6. Learn the basic theories underlying your field – By learning the groundwork that supports the work which you do, you will become much better at it. This is because you will understand why things work the way they do and what might be wrong when the things are not working fine and so on. (Quigley)

7. Look at senior developer's code – Always try and have a look at the code your senior developers are writing and ask questions like how and why things were done in a particular way. Even if other developers don't have the best coding habits, but you will still learn about how a code is written. The idea here is to understand what works and what makes sense while coding.

# Chapter 13
## Common Beginner Programming Mistakes

In this chapter, we are listing some common mistakes which are made by beginners in the programming field. These mistakes can only lead to waste of time and, therefore should be avoided.

1. <u>Messy Code formatting</u> – Beginners in programming field often make this mistake of not indenting the code properly or inconsistent use of new lines and white space. Most of the languages, like Java do not impose restrictions on how you format your code. The Java interpreter would run your code no matter how it is laid out but if the coding has proper indenting and formatting it gives it a logical structure. By spacing or tabbing code in from edge of the window, we show where loops, conditionals, and functions start and end. This way we will be sure that our code is in right place.

2. <u>Inconsistent use of lowercase and uppercase</u> – Some languages are case-sensitive and some are not, but whatever language you are writing, you should be consistent in how you use lowercase and uppercase characters in your function and variable names. Beginners in programming field often tend to make this mistake of creating a variable with one

case. For example- "var Score=6", then later reference it with a different case "if (score>2)". Also, some programmers move between different languages so as to bring the conventions of one language to another, instead of respecting the style and conventions of the new language. In JavaScript, variable and function names start with their first word with a lowercase case letter and each additional word with an uppercase letter, for e.g. myVariableName.

3. <u>Bad function and variable names</u> – Many programmers tend to abbreviate the variable name to the point that it loses all the meaning.  It is good to write longer and descriptive variable names instead of short abbreviations since it makes the intent of the code much clearer, and you are much less likely to have two different variables with the same name in different places, which can confuse you. Another common mistake which programmers do is making slang variable names which should be avoided. It is these little conventions that will save you a lot of time wondering what you called things when you go look at your old projects.

4. <u>Using a stream object without checking for fail</u> – This mistake is commonly committed by beginners and often goes unnoticed. For example-

```
int value;

while(!input.eof( ))
```

```
{
    input >> value;

    processValue( value )
}
```

The above loop is supposed to read values from an input stream and process them until it encounters the End of file. This loop works fine most of the time, but if the program encounters a non-integer in the file, then the program goes into an infinite loop. This happens because once the extractor encounters something it doesn't understand, like a character instead of a number, it sets the fail flag in the input object. Thus from that point the extractor refuses to perform any input. The worse is that the stream functions don't complain about it and the program assumes that whatever that happens to be in value was just read from the file, whereas it was just left over from a previous read.

(Davis)

1. <u>Writing functions that are too big -</u> Most of the beginners end up writing huge functions and it becomes difficult to figure out what exactly the function is supposed to do. Moreover, big functions are hard to debug since they are hard to understand, there are too many interactions and there are too many paths through the code. A function is

considered too big if it is of more than say 50 lines in length or it has more than eight if and switch statements or looping constructs. A function should be explainable in one sentence that doesn't contain AND or OR.

2. <u>Global Variables</u> – Beginners in programming field tend to declare all the variables globally. The problem will occur when the variable has a value that you didn't expect. You may think that the variable didn't get initialized because either you forgot or because the logic flow didn't go through the initialization code. You may also think that did the variable get initialized correctly? There is no exact way to tell, unless you execute the program, one section at a time while keeping an eye on other variable. There is nothing more frustrating to find out that problem on which you have been working all day goes back to global variable, changing values unexpectedly, after a call to some function that has nothing to do with that variable.

3. <u>Mishandling Exceptions</u> - In computer programming, exception handling is a great tool for handling errors but they can be misapplied. The most common error which beginners make is to catch exceptions that you never intended to. Look at the following code snippet to understand it better –

// delete the file

```
try

{

    deleteFile(filename);

}

// ignore the error if the file is not present

catch(....)

{

}
```

Here, the programmer knows that the deleteFile( ) function throws a FileNotFoundException if the file to be deleted is not present. Instead of catching that exception, programmer catches everything. Many a times, the exception is probably because the file is not there but the exception could just as well be completely unrelated. By catching and ignoring the exception, the user is unaware that the file was not deleted. (Davis)

1. Delegating to too much to frameworks – Sometimes these magic tools can lead to confusion. By abstracting functionality and assuming what we want, frameworks may leave developers at loss for what's gone wrong in their code. (Wayner, 2010)

2. Failing to maintain a program log- Another mistake which

programmer makes is not maintaining program log. A production system needs to record what it is doing, especially in case of internet-accessible systems. Most of the times a programmer only get the debug information as "it didn't work". So in such cases programmer will have to refer to the logs to tell exactly what happened. The production systems keep a constant record of what they are doing and who asked for it to be done. (Davis)

3. <u>Not validating user input</u> – Whenever a program accepts external input, it must be very careful. The program should make sure that the user input does not overflow some internal buffer and if the program uses user input to build queries, it must make sure that the said input doesn't contain controls that can leak into the query. If these basic checks are not done then your program may get hacked. Apart from this risk, you need to ensure that what you are reading is actually what you expect.

4. <u>Not using a debugger</u> – A debugger enables the programmer to go through the code in order to understand what exactly it's doing. Although this step is critical for a program not working but it is equally essential for a program that appears to be working fine. The debugger gives you more information to work with when you need a detailed understanding of what your program is doing. (Davis)

5. <u>"if" conditionals need to contain a comparison</u> – if you code

as – "if(Boolean==true)". It is one of those mistakes which actually don't do any harm, but it shows that lack of understanding of how programming language works. The brackets that come after keyword "if" must always contain a Boolean value i.e. true or false. We often compare two values in the brackets to get this Boolean. For example- "if (a <100)", in this "a<100" will resolve either true or false depending on the value of a. But if we already have a true or false value, example – "myBoolean", then we can simply write it as "if(myBoolean)" and there is no need to write "==true".

6. <u>Not backing up your work</u> - "My disk crashed" or "I lost x hours of work". These phrases should be avoided by developer. There are so many good tools for automatic back-up and version control these days. There is really no excuse to lose anything.

7. <u>Thinking you know it all</u> – Once you start writing code on your own, your confidence grows. Although it is good to feel proud about it but don't forget that you are still learning. Programmers should go back to their old code and see that which parts they have understood completely and where they have just copy-pasted.

## FAQ's

## C++

### Q.1.Before we start learning C++ is it necessary that we should have knowledge of another programming language?

**Ans:** No, it is not necessary. C++ is a simple and clear language. Although there is an intensive use of special characters like &, %,! in C++ coding but once you know the meaning of such characters it can even be more schematic and clear as compared than other languages that rely more on English words. Apart from that, the simplification of the input/output interface of C++ in comparison to C and the incorporation of the standard library in the language makes the manipulation and communication of data in a program written in C++ simple.

### Q.2Where all C++ programming language is used?

**Ans:** Various companies and government organizations use C++ programming language. There are millions of C++ users and is supported by all major vendors.

### Q.3.Who invented C++ and why?

**Ans:** C++ was invented by Bjarne Stroustrup. It was called as C++ in the year 1979. The initial version was called "C with classes" and the first version of C++ was used in AT&T in the year 1983. The first commercial implementation happened in 1985 and templates and exception handling was included later in 1980's.

Bjarne Stroustrup wanted to write efficient system programs

and to do that, he added conveniences for better data abstraction and object-oriented programming to C. The main purpose was to design a language in which developers could write programs that were both elegant and efficient.

## Q.4. What do you mean by "visual programming" and what is Visual C++?

**Ans:** Visual C++ is the name of a C++ compiler with an integrated environment from Microsoft. To simplify the development of large applications as well as specific libraries that improve productivity, Visual C++ provides special tools for it. The use of these tools is known as "visual programming".

## Q.5. Why do we need templates in C++?

**Ans:** Templates are an important part of C++ language. They allow you to develop classes or functions that are type generic; you specify the type when you use them. The library containers like algorithms and iterators are examples of generic programming. In other words, templates are the foundation of generic programming, which involves writing code in a way that is independent of any particular type. (TurtorialsPoint, 2017)

## Q.6. What is the method to link a C++ program to C functions?

**Ans:** The extern "C" linkage specification around the C function declarations is used for linking. Programmers should be aware of mangled function names and type-safe linkages.

## Q.7.What is the characteristics of class members in C++?

**Ans**: The characteristics are as follows –

a)  Functions and data are members in C++

b)  Within a class, a member cannot be re-declare

c)  Within a class definition, data members and methods must be declared

d)  In class definition, no member can be added elsewhere

## Q.8.In C++ class, what are the Access specifiers and what are their types?

**Ans**: In C++ class, Access specifiers determine the access rights for the functions or statements that follow it until the end of class or till another specifier is included. The access specifiers decide how the members of a class can be accessed. Access specifiers are of three types; private, public and protected.

## Q.9.What is the method to covert an integer to a string?

**Ans:** This new feature in C++ 11, you need to call to_string

int i =127;

string s = to_string(i);

## Q.10.Why is const variable/ const identifier better than #define?

**Ans:** #define is better than const variable/ const identifier because –

1. They are visible in debugger

2. They obey the language's scoping rules

3. You can take their address if required

4. They don't create new "keywords" in your program.

5. If you need to you can pass them by const-reference.

6. (Lavanya, 2015)

## Q.11.What is the way to initialize int with a constant?

**Ans:** There are two ways to do this –

int bar(123);

int foo = 123;

## Q.12.Do you think having lot of numbers appearing in the code is good?

**Ans:** No, in most of the cases, it's best to name your numbers appears only once in your code. Therefore, if number changes there will only be one place in the code that has to change.

## Q.13 Is it better to use void main( ) or int main( )?

**Ans:** It is better to use int main( ). Some compilers accept void main ( ), but that is not standard and should be avoided. Instead use int main( ), main( ) must return int.

**Q.14.How is copy constructor different from an overload assignment operator?**

**Ans:** An overload assignment operator assigns the content of an existing object to another existing object of the same class. Whereas, a copy constructor constructs a new object, by using the content of the argument object.

**Q.15.What is the meaning of encapsulation?**

**Ans:** Encapsulation means preventing unauthorized access to some functionality or a piece of information. It puts a firewall around the chunk (class or a group of classes), which prevents other chunks from accessing the volatile parts.

**Q.16.What is the meaning of polymorphism in C++?**

Ans: Polymorphism is the ability to call different functions by using only one type of the function call. It is referred to codes, objects or operators that behave differently in a different context. So for example, the addition function can be used in many contexts like –

- 2+2 (integer addition)

- Medical + Internship (the same operator (+) can be used with different meaning with strings.

- + 2.12 (the same operator can be used for floating point addition)

**Q.17.What is upcasting in C++ programming language?**

**Ans**: It is the act of converting a sub class references or pointer into its pointer or super class reference.

**Q.18.In C++ what is pre-processor?**

**Ans**: They are the directives, which give instructions to the compiler to pre-process the information before actual compilation starts.

**JAVA**

**Q.19.What all platforms are supported by Java programming language?**

**Ans:** Java works on various platforms, such as Mac Os, Windows and various versions of Linux/UNIX like Sun, Solaris, HP-Unix, Ubuntu, Redhat etc.

**Q.20. Why is Java a dynamic language?**

**Ans:** Java is considered as a dynamic language since it is designed to adapt to an evolving environment. Programs in Java can carry extensive amount of run-time information that can be used to verify and resolve accesses to objects on run-time. (TurtorialsPoint, 2017)

**Q.21.What is an applet?**

Ans: Applet is a Java program that runs in a web browser. It can be a fully functional Java application because it has the entire Java API at its disposal.

## Q.22.How is an applet different from a Java application?

**Ans:** As we mentioned in the previous answer, an applet runs under the control of a web browser, whereas an application runs stand-alone. Moreover, applet is subjected to more stringent restrictions in terms of network access and file, whereas an application can have free control over these resources.

## Q.23.What is the method to find out the current screen resolution in Java?

**Ans:** It is always beneficial to know about the current screen resolution, especially when you want to place a frame window in the very center of the screen. You can get the screen dimensions with the help of getScreenSize( ) method of the default screen tool kit.

## Q.24.What is the way to connect a Reader to an InputStream?

**Ans:** In Java, there aren't many PipedReaders or SocketReaders. In order to bridge the gap between Reader, and an InputStream an InputStreamReader is required.

An InputStreamReader is a reader that can be connected to any InputStream. In fact it can even be connected to filtered input streams such as BufferedInputStream or DataInputStream.

## Q.25.When should I use Reader and when should I use an InputStream?

Ans:

a. In case you are reading in text, and want to be able to call a readLine( ) method, it is better to use Readers, and particularly BufferedReaders.

b. In case you are reading data, such as bytes of information, it is best to use InputStreams, and DataInputStreams in particular.

## Q.26.What is the method to pass a primitive data type by reference?

**Ans:** All primitive data types in Java are passed by value which means that a copy is made, and that cannot be modified. When passing Java Objects, you are passing an Object reference, which makes it possible to modify the object's member variables. So if you want to pass a primitive data type by reference, you will have to wrap it in an object. However, the easiest method is to pass it as an array. The array needs to contain a single element, but wrapping it in an array means that it can be changed by a function. (Java Coffee Break)

## Q.27.What is the way to return a *null* value from an object constructor?

**Ans:** No, there is no way to return a *null* value from an object constructor because you don't return any value whatsoever from an object constructor. The object is already created and in the constructor you are just initializing the object's state. Therefore, there is no way to do it.

**Q.28.What is casting?**

**Ans:** When we explicitly convert from one primitive data type, or class to another is called as casting.

**Q.29.How can I determine the length of a string?**

**Ans:** In Java, working with strings is far easier when compared to other languages. Most programming languages represent a string as a data type, or as an array of characters. However, Java treats strings as an actual object, and provides methods that can make string manipulation easier. In Java, strings are represented by java.lang.String Class. To determine the length of a String just call the String.length( ) method, which returns an int value.

**Q.30. What is the way to call wait( ) method?**

**Ans**: The wait( ) method should always be called in loop because it's possible that until thread gets CPU to start running again the condition might not hold. Therefore, it is always better to check condition in the loop before proceeding.

**Q.31.What is the meaning of Java Beans?**

**Ans:** Components that can be used to assemble a large Java application are called as Java Beans. Beans are classes that have properties, and can trigger events. In order to define a property, a bean author provides accessor methods, which can get and set the value of a property. Bean tool should inspect the class for methods matching the get/set pattern and should also allow modifying the object's properties. (Java Coffee Break)

## Q.32.In Java, what is the difference between StringBuilder and StringBuffer?

**Ans:** The StringBuilder is introduced in Java5 and difference between StringBuilder and StringBuffer is that; StringBuilder methods are non-synchronized, whereas StringBuffer methods are synchronized.

## Q.33. When do you override equals ( ) and hashcode?

**Ans:** You can override whenever it is necessary, especially if you want to use your object as key in HashMap or you want to do equality check.

## Q.34. What do you understand by Singleton Pattern?

**Ans:** A Singleton Pattern is a design pattern that restricts the instantiation of a class to one object. It is useful when exactly one object is needed to coordinate actions across the system. (Shafaet)

## SQL
## Q.35.How many statements are there in SQL?

**Ans:** There are three statements in SQL, they are –

a) Data Definition Language or DDL – It is used to define the structure that holds the data. Example – Alter, Drop, Create, table and Truncate.

b) Data Manipulation Language or DML– It is used for manipulation of data itself. DML's typical operations are Delete, Insert, Update and retrieving data from the table.

345

The Select statements cannot change the data in the database, hence they are considered as limited version of DML. However, it can perform operations on data that is retrieved from the DBMS, before the results are returned to the calling function.

c) Data Control Language or DCL - It is used to control the visibility of data like granting database access and set privileges to create tables etc. For example – Grant, Revoke access permission to user in order to access data in database.

(Chaudhary, 2015)

## Q.36. What is the meaning of DBMS?

**Ans:** It is the database management system, which is a collection of programs that enables user to store, update, delete and retrieve information from database.

## Q.37. What is the difference between MySQL or SQL server and SQL?

**Ans:** The Structured Query Language or SQL is a language that communicates with a relational database thus providing ways of creating and manipulating the databases. Microsoft's SQL Server and MySQL both are relational database management systems that use SQL as their standard relational database language.

## Q.38. What is the difference between DELETE, TRUNCATE and DROP commands?

**Ans:** DELETE – This command is used to remove all or some rows from a table. A WHRE clause can be used to remove some tables and if no WHERE clause is specified then all the rows will be removed. Once you perform the DELETE command, you need to COMMIT or ROLLBACK the transaction to make it permanent or to undo it. Important point to note is that this operation will cause all DELETE triggers to fire.

TRUNCATE- this command is used to remove all the rows from a table. TRUNCATE command cannot be rolled back and no triggers will be fired. It is faster than the DELETE command and it doesn't use as much undo space as a DELETE.

DROP – this command removes the table from the database. It removes all the tables' indexes, rows and privileges. The operation cannot be rolled back and no triggers will be fired.

## Q.39.Can we select a random collection of rows from a table?

Ans: Yes, we can do by following methods –

a) SAMPLE Clause- The simple way to randomly select rows from a table is to use SAMPLE clause with a SELECT statement. For example –

SELECT * FROM emp SAMPLE(5);

Oracle is instructed to randomly return 5% of the rows in the table.

a) ORDER BY dbms_random.value() – this method orders the data by a random column number. For example –

SQL> SELECT * FROM (SELECT ename

2       FROM emp

3       ORDER BY dbms_random.value( ) )

4  WHERE rownum <= 3;

ENAME

  --------------------------

  WARD

  MILLER

  TURNER

## Q.40. What is the method to add a column to the middle of the table?

**Ans:** The columns in Oracle can be added only at the end of the existing table. However, some databases also allow columns to be added to an existing table after a particular column. In the below example, the Syntax is valid in MySQL-

ALTER TABLE tablename ADD columnname AFTER columnname;

However, Oracle does not support this syntax, but that does not mean that it cannot be done. There are workarounds methods to do this –

a) Create a new table and copy the data across.

b) Rename the table and create a view upon it with its former name and with the columns in the order you want.

c) Use the DBMS_REDEFINITION package to change the structure online while users are working.

## Q.41. What is the meaning of Database lock and what types of locks are there?

**Ans:** The database lock tells a transaction, if the data item in question is currently being used by other transactions. Types of locks –

a) Shared Lock- When it is applied on data item, other transactions can only read the item, but can't write into it.

b) Exclusive Lock – When this lock is applied on data item, other transactions can't read or write into the data item.

(Chaudhary, 2015)

## Q.42. What is a composite Key?

**Ans:** It is a type of candidate key, which represents set columns whose values uniquely identify each row in a table. (Chaudhary, 2015)

## Q.43. What is the difference between unique key and primary key?

**Ans:** Both primary key and unique key enforces uniqueness of the column on which they are defined. Unique key creates a non-clustered index by default, whereas primary key creates clustered index on the column. Another difference is that, unique key allows only one NULL, whereas primary key doesn't allow NULLs. (Dave, 2008)

## Q.44. When and where should we use wild cards in database for Pattern Matching?

Ans: The SQL Like operator is used for pattern matching. The 'Like' command takes more time to process so before using it, you may consider the following points on when and where to use wild card search.

a) Do not overuse wild card. In case another search operator can do then use it instead of wild card.

b) Try not to use wild cards at the beginning of the search pattern, unless it is extremely necessary. Search patterns that begin wild cards are the slowest to process.

c) Pay attention to the placement of wild card symbols because if they are misplaced, you might not return the intended data.

(Chaudhary, 2015)

## Q.45.What do we understand by stored procedure and what are its uses?

Ans: A function that contains a collection of SQL queries is called as a stored procedure. The procedure can take inputs, process them and send back the output. Stored procedures are precompiled and stored in the database which enables the database to execute the queries much faster. As we can include many queries in a stored procedure, round trip time to execute multiple queries from source code to database and back is avoided. (Chaudhary, 2015)

## Q.46.Is it possible to link SQL servers to other servers like Oracle?

Ans: Yes, SQL server can be linked to any server provided it has OLE-DB provider from Microsoft to allow a link.

## Q.47. What do you understand by SQL server agent?

Ans: SQL server agent plays an important role in day to day tasks of a database administrator. Its purpose is to ease the implementation of tasks for DBA (database administrator), with its full function scheduling engine, that allows you to schedule your own scripts and jobs.

## Q.48. What are the different types of indexes?

Ans: There are three types of indexes –

a) Clustered Index – It reorders the physical order of the table and search based on the key values. Each table can have only one clustered index.

b) Non-Clustered Index- It does not alter the physical order of the table and maintains the logical order of data. Each table can have 999 non-clustered indexes.

c) Unique Index- This type of index does not allow the field to have duplicate values if the column is unique indexed. The Unique index can be applied automatically when primary key is defined.

(Chaudhary, 2015)

**Q.49. What is database relationship?**

Ans: The database relationship is defined as the connection between the tables in a database. There are four database relationships; one to one relationship, one to many relationship, many to one relationship and self-referencing relationship.

**Q.50. Which operator is used in query for pattern matching?**

**Ans:** The LIKE operator is used for pattern matching. It can be used as follows –

a) % - match zero or more characters

b) Underscore ( _ ) – matching exactly one character.

# Glossary of Common Programming Terms

There are a large number of terms that you will come across in your programming but the following are the most common and the ones that you need to learn in order to get started:

## Compiler

The program that converts your written code into computer language so that it can be executed

## Database

A file that holds information in a structured manner, similar in many ways to a spreadsheet. These are used to store data in and to enable you to retrieve that data for the program to use

## Algorithm

A set of steps or instructions that are used in solving a problem. If you are asked how to do something, you told that person to "do this, the do this, and then do that, and if you see this, you should do that" you have basically given them an algorithm. This is the kind of thing that computers use to gain results based on the data that is contained in the program.

## Object Oriented

OOP or Object Oriented Programming is fairly recent in

computer programming languages, basically a new design on the way that programmers think about how they are going to solve a particular problem. Instead of using the tried and tested method of functions and algorithms, you think instead about each "object" in the program and what it needs to do. As a beginner, you do not need to worry too much about the concepts of OOP – the time for leaning them will become clear as you work your way up the ladder as a programmer.

## Platform

A platform is the specific type of operating system and hardware that you are creating a program for. The most common ones are Windows, Mac, iOS and Android.

# Conclusion

I hope that you found my introduction of computer programming helpful. It is a very basic start but it should have given you some idea on how to begin. It should also have shown you that computer programming really isn't all that difficult ad can be quite exciting, especially as you start to see your results appear on screen and see your computer, in short, doing what it is told to do!

If you found that this has given you a good idea of what to expect then you may want to move on to more advanced programming in your chosen language. A word of warning here – do not try to learn more than one language at a time, otherwise you will find yourself in a muddle. The only other piece of advice I will give you at this stage is to practice...and keep on practicing. The more you do the more you will learn, and the more you will want to learn.

Thank you for downloading my book; if you found it helpful please consider leaving me a review at Amazon.com.

# Thank you

Thank you very much for taking your time and reading through the book. I hope this book had tremendous value for you and helped you to master the basics of C++, SQL, & Java-Programming.

Out of all the C++, SQL, & Java -Programming related books you chose this book.

Thank you very much again for giving it a chance. It's now time to take what you just learned into action!

At this part I'd like to ask you for a 'little' favor. May it be possible to leave a review for this guide on Amazon?

1 star – I really didn't like it

2 stars – it was okay

3 stars – I enjoyed it but it wasn't the best

4 stars – I really enjoyed it

5 stars – I LOVED it

Your review and feedback means a lot to us. Based on your feedback we can evaluate what you liked and what we can improve. Let us know how we can help you becoming a master programmer. On behalf of Joseph Connor we from MJGPublishing are deeply grateful.

Last but not least, receive the latest information on programming by subscribing to our newsletter: https://www.mjgpublishing.com/newsletter

Contact us at MJGPublishing at any time: marco@mjgpublishing.com

# Bibliography

Arora, R. (2014, February 12). *What's teh difference between declaring finctions before or after main()?* Retrieved from Stack Overflow: http://www.copyscape.com/viewfound.php?o=95324&t=14873 42363&z=94752&sh=1#copyscape_start

Batra, J. (2016, October 22). *C & C Training in Ambala? Batra Computer Centre.* Retrieved from Slide Share: http://www.slideshare.net/seowale1/c-c-training-in-ambala-batra-computer-centre

Chaudhary, A. (2015, February 26). *Dbms interview questions.* Retrieved from Slideshare: http://www.slideshare.net/ambika93/dbms-interview-questions

Dave, P. (2008, September 14). *SQL SERVER - 2008- Interview Questions and Answers- Part 3.* Retrieved from SQL Authority: https://blog.sqlauthority.com/2008/09/14/sql-server-2008-interview-questions-and-answers-part-3/

Davis, S. R. (n.d.). *The 10 Most Common Beginner Programming Mistakes.* Retrieved February 17, 2017, from dummies: http://www.dummies.com/programming/cpp/the-10-most-common-beginner-programming-mistakes/

Gananathan, V. (n.d.). *Venkatash SQL Intro.* Retrieved February 16, 2017, from Advantages and Disadvantages:

http://www.cs.iit.edu/~cs561/cs425/VenkatashSQLIntro/Adva
ntages%20&%20Disadvantages.html

james, J. (2009, May 21). *10 tips for advancing from a beginner
to an intermediate developer*. Retrieved from Tech Republic:
http://www.techrepublic.com/blog/10-things/10-tips-for-
advancing-from-a-beginner-to-an-intermediate-developer/

Java Coffee Break. (n.d.). *What Exactly are Java Beans.*
Retrieved February 17, 2017, from Java Coffee Break:
http://www.javacoffeebreak.com/faq/faq0003.html

Java T Point. (n.d.). *PL/SQL Function*. Retrieved February 17,
2017, from Java T Point: http://www.javatpoint.com/pl-sql-
function

Lavanya, B. (2015, October 30). *Learning c++*. Retrieved from
Slideshare: http://www.slideshare.net/balalavanya9/learning-
c-54553311

Quigley, A. (n.d.). *ood coder or Great Coder? From beginner, to
intermediate, to expert*. Retrieved Februrary 17, 2017, from
Code Institute: http://www.techrepublic.com/blog/10-
things/10-tips-for-advancing-from-a-beginner-to-an-
intermediate-developer/

R4R. (n.d.). *R4R*. Retrieved February 16, 2017, from R4R Right
Place for the Right Person: http://r4r.co.in/sql/

Rider, J. (2005, February 21). *Java REserved Identifiers.*

Retrieved February 16, 2017, from Jwrider:
http://www.jwrider.com/riderist/java/javaidrs.htm

Ringer, C. (2016, February 6). *String Field Length in Postres SQL*. Retrieved February 16, 2017, from Stack Overflow:
http://www.copyscape.com/viewfound.php?o=50045&t=14872 93584&z=106792&sh=1#copyscape_start

Shafaet. (n.d.). *Java Singleton Pattern*. Retrieved February 17, 2017, from Hacker Rank:
https://www.hackerrank.com/challenges/java-singleton

Singh, C. (n.d.). *C Keywords - Reserved Words*. Retrieved February 16, 2017, from Beginner's Book:
http://beginnersbook.com/2014/01/c-keywords-reserved-words/

*SQL Wildcards*. (n.d.). Retrieved from w3schools.com:
https://www.w3schools.com/sql/sql_wildcards.asp

Tandukar, F. (2014, February 28). *Function in c*. Retrieved from Slide Share: http://www.slideshare.net/rktandukar/function-in-c-31782897

Thakker, M. (2016, October 20). *Quora*. Retrieved February 16, 2017, from What are the Best Sides of Java Project?:
https://www.quora.com/What-are-the-best-sides-of-Java-project

Toal, R. (2010, May 2). *Programming Language Design*

*Sketchbook*. Retrieved February 16, 2017, from Blogpost.com: http://language-design.blogspot.com/2010/05/reserved-words.html

TurtorialsPoint. (2017). *Computer Programming - Quick Guide.* Retrieved February 16, 2017, from TutorialsPoint: https://www.tutorialspoint.com/computer_programming/com puter_programming_quick_guide.htm

Wayner, P. (2010, December 6). *12 programming mistakes to avoid.* Retrieved from InfoWorld: http://www.infoworld.com/article/2624898/application-development/12-programming-mistakes-to-avoid.html

YURI56. (2013, December 10). *File and Stream in Java.* Retrieved from Slideshare: http://www.slideshare.net/yuri56/file-and-stream-in-java

# Free Video Course: Introduction to JavaScript, SQL & C++

I really hope that you enjoyed the book! You are now familiar with the first steps on Computer Programming. It's now time to take action!

Click the below image or link to get immediate access:

Click this link: **http://www.mjgpublishing.com/free-programming-course NOW** and get immediate access to your free video series!

# Check Out My Other Books
# Want to Learn more about
# Programming?

Check out the other books by Joseph Connor:

**Newest release (2017): Programming: Computer Programming For Beginners: Learn the Basics of SQL**

**C#: Computer Programming for Beginners: Learn the Basics of C Sharp Programming – 3rd Edition (2017)**

Programming: Computer Programming For Beginners: Learn The Basics Of HTML5, JavaScript, & CSS

Python: The Definitive Guide to Learning Python Programming for Beginners

**Hacking: Hacking for Beginners - Computer Virus, Cracking, Malware, IT Security**

Check out our **Facebook** and **Instagram** to receive updates on the newest releases!

Made in the USA
San Bernardino, CA
14 June 2017